UNVEILING MAYA

Translation and Hidden Insights of Dakshinamurthi Stotram

RAJEEV KURAPATI

ISBN 979-8-89133-906-4

TABLE OF CONTENTS

Rajeev Kurapati's 'Unveiling Maya' is an excellent translation and commentary on Adi Shankaracharya's Sri Dakshinamurthy Stotram. This stotram is distinctive in the sense that it drips with intense devotion to the Ishvara in the form of Dakshinamurthy and at the same time enunciates deep philosophical insights unveiling the reality of the Self.

Kurapati's commentary rightly recognises this two-fold aspect of the Stotram. While the major focus of the book is on philosophical insights of the Stotram which it beautifully captures, the whole teaching is grounded in an enunciation of who Dakshinamurthy is, right at the very beginning of the book. Another notable feature of the book is its adoption of commentary format for enunciation. This ensures a continuity with ancient tradition all the while also contemporizing those teachings.

I congratulate the author for bringing out this handy manual on Vedanta.

– Nithin Sridhar

Author, Vedanta Seeker, and Director, Indica Moksha

ACKNOWLEDGEMENTS

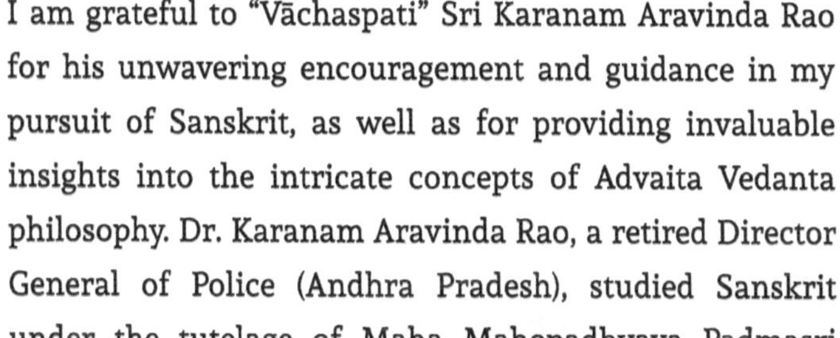

I am grateful to "Vāchaspati" Sri Karanam Aravinda Rao for his unwavering encouragement and guidance in my pursuit of Sanskrit, as well as for providing invaluable insights into the intricate concepts of Advaita Vedanta philosophy. Dr. Karanam Aravinda Rao, a retired Director General of Police (Andhra Pradesh), studied Sanskrit under the tutelage of Maha Mahopadhyaya Padmasri Dr. Sri Pullela Sriramachandrudu and studied Vedanta under the mentorship of Maha Mahopadhyaya Swami Tattvavidananda Saraswati.

Sri Aravinda Rao has done valuable service in promoting Sanskrit, while his discourses on various topics like Bhagavad Gita, Upanishads, and other works on Vedanta weave ancient wisdom with practical knowledge.

I am incredibly fortunate to have him as my mentor.

INTRODUCTION

On a crisp morning, an inquisitive 16-year-old boy approached his grandfather, his mind ablaze with a relentless question that refused to let go. "Grandpa," he began, "I've watched you offer your prayers each morning, but I can't help but wonder, who is it that you're praying to?" The grandfather, a venerable 67-year-old, met his grandson's inquiry with a smile. "I pray to God," he replied simply. Undeterred by the response, the boy persisted. "I know you pray to God. But what is God, Grandpa? Where can we find God, and what does God look like?"

The grandfather, feeling a touch of irritation, responded, "My dear grandson, in all my years, I've never questioned God. I've faithfully followed our tradition (sampradāya), performed my religious duties, and I've been blessed with a good life. I'm content with that. My advice to you is to do the same, to follow our tradition without questioning them. You're only 16, and some questions are best left unasked."

Disillusioned by his grandfather's response, the boy resolved to embark on a quest for answers elsewhere. His curiosity burgeoned, driven by a thirst for understanding the mysteries of existence—questions about life after death, our origin before birth, and beyond. With determination, he headed to the local temple, where he posed the same earnest inquiry to the priest. To his disappointment, the priest's response echoed his grandfather's, urging him to embrace tradition and refrain from delving too deeply into the unfathomable depths of the divine.

As the years passed, he reluctantly set aside his pressing questions, engaging fully in the busyness of life's journey. Yet, one couldn't help but wonder if those queries would resurface someday, leading him on a journey to uncover the profound mysteries of life.

Could that boy be you, dear reader, poised on the cusp of your own quest for understanding in the tapestry of existence?

In the vast expanse of philosophical traditions originating from ancient India, there lies a gem that has illuminated the hearts and minds of seekers of spiritual knowledge—the Dakṣiṇāmūrti Stotram. This sacred chant, a profound tribute to the mystical teacher Dakṣiṇāmūrti, revered as a manifestation of Lord Shiva, transcends mere words; it serves as an entryway to the profound depths of spiritual wisdom.

The Dakṣiṇāmūrti stotram isn't just a hymn singing praises to the divine; it's a journey into profound philosophy. It ventures deep into the heart of reality by dispelling the illusion of duality.

Unveiling Māya: Translation and Hidden Insights of Dakṣiṇāmūrti Stotram is not merely a translation of this ancient text but an exploration, a journey into its very essence. Each verse carries with it layers of meaning, hidden insights that have, over time, been overshadowed by ritualistic recitations. This book aims to peel back these layers, revealing the profound wisdom embedded within.

The Dakṣiṇāmūrti Stotram is unique in that it delves into philosophy, metaphysics, and the very nature of existence. It speaks of the world, the play of Māya (illusion), the nature of the Self, and the role of the Guru.

As we embark on this journey, we will delve into a word-to-word translation of the Stotram, ensuring that even those new to the text can grasp its essence. But more than that, we will dive deep into its hidden insights, exploring commentaries from ancient seers and briefly connecting them to modern understandings.

In essence, this book is an invitation. An invitation to immerse oneself in the timeless wisdom of the

Dakṣiṇāmūrti Stotram, to reflect, to meditate, and to emerge with a deeper understanding of oneself and the universe.

Chapter One provides an introductory overview, unraveling the core themes and fundamental concepts found in the Dakṣiṇāmūrti Stotram.

Chapter Two delves into the profound spiritual significance of the Dakṣiṇāmūrti Stotram within Vedanta traditions. Additionally, this chapter explores the intricate symbolism and metaphors interwoven throughout the Stotram.

Chapter Three delves deep into the principles of Advaita Vedanta, shedding light on the significance of Guru Dakṣiṇāmūrti. It offers an accessible explanation of key Vedantic concepts: Jīva, Atma, Jagat, and Brahman, along with their interrelatedness. The concept of Maya is elucidated, and the three orders of reality according to Advaita Vedanta are discussed.

Chapter Four introduces readers to the primary commentaries associated with the Dakṣiṇāmūrti Stotram, shedding light on the commentaries that have significantly shaped our understanding of this revered composition.

Chapter Five presents a transliteration of the Stotram's Sanskrit verses, followed by a comprehensive line-by-line translation and commentary. This section offers readers a lucid comprehension of the Stotram's verses and their profound meanings.

Embark on this sacred journey hand in hand with the divine teacher, Dakṣiṇāmūrti, as we unlock the wisdom that has enlightened sages and seekers throughout the ages.

Sanskrit Text and English Transliteration of the Dakṣiṇāmūrti Stotram

शान्तिपाठः

śāntipāṭhaḥ

ॐ यो ब्रह्माणं विदधाति पूर्वम्
यो वै वेदांश्च प्रहिणोति तस्मै ।
तं ह देवमात्मबुद्धिप्रकाशं
मुमुक्षुर्वै शरणमहं प्रपद्ये ॥
ॐ शान्तिः शान्तिः शान्तिः

Om yo brahmāṇaṁ vidadhāti pūrvam

yo vai vedāṁśca prahiṇoti tasmai |

taṁ ha devamātmabuddhiprakāśaṁ

mumukṣurvai śaraṇamahaṁ prapadye ||

ध्यानश्लोका

Dhyānaślokāḥ

मौनव्याख्याप्रकटितपरब्रह्मतत्त्वं युवानं
वर्षिष्ठान्ते वसदृषिगणैरावृतं ब्रह्मनिष्ठैः ।
आचार्येन्द्रं करकलितचिन्मुद्रमानन्दरूपं
स्वात्मारामं मुदितवदनं दक्षिणामूर्तिमीडे ॥ १॥

Mounavyākhyāprakaṭitaparabrahmatattvaṃ yuvānaṃ

Varṣiṣṭhānte vasadṛṣigaṇairāvṛtaṃ brahmaniṣṭhaiḥ I

Ācāryendraṃ karakalitachinmudramānandarūpaṃ

Swātmārāmaṃ muditavādanaṃ dakṣiṇāmūrtimīḍe II 1 II

वटविटपिसमीपे भूमिभागे निषण्णं
सकलमुनिजनानां ज्ञानदातारमारात् ।
त्रिभुवनगुरुमीशं दक्षिणामूर्तिदेवं
जननमरणदुःखच्छेददक्षं नमामि ॥ २ ॥

vaṭaviṭapisamīpe bhūmibhāge niṣaṇṇam

sakalamunijanānāṃ jñānadātāramārāt I

tribhuvanagurumīśam dakṣiṇāmūrtidevaṃ

jananamaraṇaduḥkhacchedadakṣam namāmi II 2 II

चित्रं वटतरोर्मूले वृद्धाः शिष्या गुरुर्युवा ।
गुरोऽस्तु मौनं व्याख्यानं शिष्यास्तु छिन्न संशयाः ॥ ३॥

chitraṃ vaṭatarormūle vṛddhāḥ śiṣyā gururyuvā

guro'stu maunaṃ vyākhyānaṃ śiṣyāstu chinna saṃśayāḥ II 3 II

निधये सर्वविद्यानां भिषजे भवरोगिणाम् ।
गुरवे सर्वलोकानां दक्षिणामूर्तये नमः ॥ ४॥

Nidhaye sarvavidyānāṁ bhiṣaje bhavaroginām |

Gurave sarvalokānāṁ dakṣiṇāmūrtaye namaḥ II 4 II

ॐ नमः प्रणवार्थाय शुद्धज्ञानैकमूर्तये ।
निर्मलाय प्रशान्ताय दक्षिणामूर्तये नमः ॥ ५॥

Om namaḥ praṇavārthāya śuddhajñānaikamūrtaye |

Nirmalāya praśāntāya dakṣiṇāmūrtaye namaḥ II 5 II

दक्षिणामूर्तिस्तोत्रं
Dakṣiṇāmūrti Stotram

विश्वं दर्पणदृश्यमाननगरीतुल्यं निजान्तर्गतं
पश्यन्नात्मनि मायया बहिरिवोद्भूतं यथा निद्रया।
यः साक्षात्कुरुते प्रबोधसमये स्वात्मानमेवाद्वयं
तस्मै श्रीगुरुमूर्तये नम इदं श्रीदक्षिणामूर्तये ॥ १ ॥

viśvaṁ darpaṇadṛśyamānanagarītulyaṁ nijāntargataṁ

paśyannātmani māyayā bahirivodbhūtaṁ yathā nidrayā I

yaḥ sākṣātkurute prabodhasamaye svātmānamevādvayaṁ

tasmai śrīgurumūrtaye nama idaṁ śrīdakṣiṇāmūrtaye II 1 II

बीजस्यान्तरिवाङ्कुरो जगदिदं प्राङ्निर्विकल्पं पुनः
मायाकल्पितदेशकालकलनावैचित्र्यचित्रीकृतम् ।
मायावीव विजृम्भयत्यपि महायोगीव यः स्वेच्छया
तस्मै श्रीगुरुमूर्तये नम इदं श्रीदक्षिणामूर्तये ॥ २ ॥

bījasyāntarivaṅkuro jagadidaṃ prāṅnirvikalpaṃ punaḥ

māyākalpitadeśakālakalanāvaicitryacitrīkṛtam

māyāvīva vijṛmbhayatyapi mahāyogīva yaḥ svechchayā

tasmai śrīgurumūrtaye nama idaṃ śrīdakṣiṇāmūrtaye II 2 II

यस्यैव स्फुरणं सदात्मकमसत्कल्पार्थकं भासते
साक्षात्तत्त्वमसीति वेदवचसा यो बोधयत्याश्रितान् ।
यत्साक्षात्करणाद्भवेन्न पुनरावृत्तिर्भवाम्भोनिधौ
तस्मै श्रीगुरुमूर्तये नम इदं श्रीदक्षिणामूर्तये ॥ ३ ॥

yasyaiva sphuraṇaṃ sadātmakam asat kalpārthakaṃ bhāsate

sākṣāttattvamasi iti vedavacasā yo bodhayaty āśritān |

yatsākṣātkaraṇādbhavenna punarāvṛttirbhavāmbhonidhau

tasmai śrīgurumūrtaye nama idaṃ śrīdakṣiṇāmūrtaye || 3 ||

नानाच्छिद्रघटोदरस्थितमहादीपप्रभाभास्वरं
ज्ञानं यस्य तु चक्षुरादिकरणद्वारा बहिः स्पन्दते ।
जानामीति तमेव भान्तमनुभात्येतत्समस्तं जगत्
तस्मै श्रीगुरुमूर्तये नम इदं श्रीदक्षिणामूर्तये ॥४॥

nānāchchhidraghaṭodarasthitamahādīpprabhā bhāsvaraṃ

jñānaṃ yasya tu cakṣurādikaraṇadvāra bahiḥ spandate I

jānāmīti tameva bhāntamanubhātyetatsamastaṃ jagat

tasmai śrīgurumūrtaye nama idaṃ śrīdakṣiṇāmūrtaye II 4 II

देहं प्राणमपीन्द्रियाण्यपि चलां बुद्धिं च शून्यं विदुः
स्त्रीबालान्धजडोपमास्त्वहमिति भ्रान्ता भृशं वादिनः ।
मायाशक्तिविलासकल्पितमहाव्यामोहसंहारिणे
तस्मै श्रीगुरुमूर्तये नम इदं श्रीदक्षिणामूर्तये ॥५॥

deham prāṇamapīndriyāṇyapi calāṁ buddhiṁ ca śūnyaṁ viduḥ

strībālāndhajaḍopamāstvahamiti bhrāntā bhṛśaṁ vādinaḥ I

māyāśaktivilāsakalpitamahāvyāmohasaṁhāriṇe

tasmai śrīgurumūrtaye nama idaṁ śrīdakṣiṇāmūrtaye II 5 II

राहुग्रस्तदिवाकरेन्दुसदृशो मायासमाच्छादनात्
सन्मात्रः करणोपसंहरणतो योऽभूत्सुषुप्तः पुमान् ।
प्रागस्वाप्समिति प्रबोधसमये यः प्रत्यभिज्ञायते
तस्मै श्रीगुरुमूर्तये नम इदं श्रीदक्षिणामूर्तये ॥ ६॥

Rāhugrastadivākarendusadṛśo māyāsamācchādanāt

Sanmātraḥ karaṇopasaṁharaṇato yo'bhūtsuṣuptaḥ pumān |

Prāgasvāpsamiti prabodhasamaye yaḥ pratyabhijñāyate

Tasmai śrīgurumūrtaye nama idaṁ śrīdakṣiṇāmūrtaye II 6 II

बाल्यादिष्वपि जाग्रदादिषु तथा सर्वास्ववस्थास्वपि
व्यावृत्तास्वनुवर्तमानमहमित्यन्तः स्फुरन्तं सदा ।
स्वात्मानं प्रकटीकरोति भजतां यो मुद्रयाभद्रया
तस्मै श्रीगुरुमूर्तये नम इदं श्रीदक्षिणामूर्तये ॥७॥

Bālyādiṣvapi jāgradādiṣu tathā sarvāsvavasthāsvapi

Vyāvṛttāsvanuvartamānamahamityantaḥ sphurantaṁ sadā I

Svātmānaṁ prakaṭīkaroti bhajatāṁ yo mudrayābhadrayā

Tasmai śrīgurumūrtaye nama idaṁ śrīdakṣiṇāmūrtaye II7II

विश्वं पश्यति कार्यकारणतया स्वस्वामिसम्बन्धतः
शिष्याचार्यतया तथैव पितृपुत्राद्यात्मना भेदतः।
स्वप्ने जाग्रति वा य एष पुरुषो मायापरिभ्रामितः
तस्मै श्रीगुरुमूर्तये नम इदं श्रीदक्षिणामूर्तये ॥८॥

Viśvaṁ paśyati kāryakāraṇatayā svasvāmisambandhataḥ

śiṣyācāryatayā tathaiva pitṛputrādyātmanā bhedataḥ I

Svapne jāgrati vā ya eṣa puruṣo māyāparibhrāmitaḥ

Tasmai śrīgurumūrtaye nama idaṁ śrīdakṣiṇāmūrtaye II 8 II

भूरम्भांस्यनलोऽनिलोऽम्बरमहर्नाथो हिमांशु पुमान्
इत्याभाति चराचरात्मकमिदं यस्यैव मूर्त्यष्टकम्
नान्यत् किञ्चन विद्यते विमृशतां यस्मात्परस्माद्विभोः
तस्मै श्रीगुरुमूर्तये नम इदं श्रीदक्षिणामूर्तये ॥९॥

Bhūrambhāṁsyanalo'nilo'ambaramaharnātho himāṁshu pumān

ityābhāti carācarātmakamidaṁ yasyaiva mūrtyaṣṭakam

nānyat kiñcana vidyate vimṛśatāṁ yasmātparasmādvibhoḥ

tasmai śrīgurumūrtaye nama idaṁ śrīdakṣiṇāmūrtaye II 9 II

सर्वात्मत्वमिति स्फुटीकृतमिदं यस्मादमुष्मिन् स्तवे
तेनास्य श्रवणात्तदर्थमननाद्ध्यानाच्च संकीर्तनात् ।
सर्वात्मत्वमहाविभूतिसहितं स्यादीश्वरत्वं स्वतः
सिद्ध्येत्तत्पुनरष्टधा परिणतं चैश्वर्यमव्याहतम् ॥१०॥

Sarvātmatvamiti sphuṭīkṛtamidaṁ yasmādamuṣmin stave

tenāsya śravaṇāttadarthamananāddhyānācca saṅkīrtanāt I

Sarvātmatvamahāvibhūtisahitaṁ syādīśvaratvaṁ svataḥ

siddhyettatpunaraṣṭadhā pariṇataṁ caiśvaryamavyāhatam II 10 II

Chapter 1

Dakṣiṇāmūrti Stotram Overview

Who is Dakṣiṇāmūrti?

Dakṣiṇāmūrti, a form of Lord Shiva, is elaborated more within the Shaiva traditions and āgami (canonical) texts rather than the Vedas, ancient Indian texts that form the foundation of Hindu spiritual, ritualistic, and philosophical knowledge. The term "Dakṣiṇāmūrti" literally means "one whose form is facing south," and there are deep symbolisms associated with this direction and the form of Shiva.

दक्षिणामूर्तिः (Dakṣiṇāmūrtih) can be understood as दक्षिणाभिमुखा मूर्तिः (Dakṣiṇābhimukhā murtih). The compound दक्षिणाभिमुखा मूर्तिः (Dakṣiṇābhimukhā murtih) means:

- दक्षिणा (Dakṣiṇā) means, south

- अभिमुखा (Abhimukhā) means, facing towards or oriented

- मूर्तिः (Mūrtih) means, form or idol

The compound दक्षिणाभिमुखा मूर्तिः can be translated as, the form or idol that is facing south.

Grammatically, this compound word is a बहुव्रीहि समास (Bahuvrīhi samāsa). In a Bahuvrīhi compound, the entire compound word acts as an adjective to describe something external to the word itself. The meaning of the compound word is not directly related to the individual meanings of its components but describes something that possesses the qualities mentioned in the compound. In this case, the compound word describes a form that faces the south.

दक्षिणामूर्तिः (Dakṣiṇāmūrtiḥ) can also be explained, grammatically, as a कर्मधारय समास (Karmadhāraya samāsa), as दक्षिणश्चासौ अमूर्तिश्चः (Dakṣiṇaścāsau Amūrtiśca), which can be broken down as:

- दक्षिणः (Dakṣiṇaḥ) – In this context, this term is interpreted as दक्षः (Dakṣaḥ), which refers to someone who is adept, skilled, or proficient. The term सिद्धः (siddhaḥ) is used to explain the significance of दक्षः (Dakṣaḥ). सिद्धः (siddhaḥ) means someone who has achieved mastery or perfection in a particular field or discipline or refers to someone who has attained a certain level of spiritual realization or enlightenment. The dhatu (root) for सिद्धः (siddhaḥ) is सिद्ध (sidh), means, to attain, to succeed, or to accomplish.

- च (ca) – and

- असौ (Asau) – that person or he

- अमूर्तिः (Amūrtiḥ) – formless
- च (ca) – and

In the compound word formation known as Karmadhāraya samāsa, the first component can function as an adjective to the second, or both components can share the same grammatical case (विभक्ति, vibhakti), with neither modifying the other. This type of compound word in Sanskrit is descriptive of a form, person or a character using adjectives and typically has the sense of "and", connecting the two components. Here, both words (Dakṣaḥ and Amūrtiḥ) stand in an appositional relationship, meaning they refer to the same entity. This is called सामानाधिकरणम् (sāmānādhikaraṇam).

In the context of Karmadhāraya samāsa, सामानाधिकरणम् (sāmānādhikaraṇam) refers to the situation where both words in the compound have a co-reference to the same entity. In simpler terms, in a Karmadhāraya samāsa exhibiting sāmānādhikaraṇam, the first word provides a description or qualification for the second word, and both words point back to the same referent or entity.

Given this, the compound दक्षिणामूर्तिः (Dakṣiṇāmūrtiḥ) can be expanded as "He who is skillful or expert and is formless". This interpretation aligns with the concept of Dakṣiṇāmūrti as Lord Shiva in his form as the supreme teacher, embodying supreme knowledge and skill while also representing the formless reality.

There's more to this name in its spiritual context. "Dakshina" is a multifaceted term in Sanskrit, and its meaning can vary based on the context in which it's used:

1. Directional Meaning: In its most basic sense, "Dakshina" means "south."

2. Ritualistic Offering: In many Vedanta rituals, especially during the performance of yajnas (sacrificial rituals) or during the ceremony of a guru-disciple initiation, "Dakshina" refers to a gift or offering given to a priest or a teacher as a token of gratitude. This is usually a voluntary act and signifies respect, gratitude, and acknowledgment of the services rendered.

3. Benevolence: In certain contexts, "Dakshina" also symbolizes benevolence or favorableness.

The act of giving "Dakshina" is considered an essential aspect of dharma (righteous duty) in many traditional rituals and ceremonies, ensuring the reciprocation of energy and gratitude between the giver and the receiver.

Dakṣiṇāmūrti, while the name literally refers to "the one with a form facing south," there's a deeper spiritual symbolism where "Dakshina" signifies the benevolent and gracious form of the teacher who imparts wisdom.

The term "murti" in Sanskrit primarily refers to a form, embodiment, or manifestation. In a religious and spiritual context, "murti" is often used to denote an idol or a representation of a deity used for worship in temples or homes. This representation can be sculpted in stone, metal, clay, or other materials.

It's important to note that in Vedanta philosophy, a murti is not just an "idol" in the sense of being an inanimate object; it's considered a tangible manifestation of the divine (Ishvara), a conduit through which devotees can connect with the deity. Through rituals of consecration, the divine essence is invoked into the murti, making it sacred and a focal point for devotion.

So, "murti" signifies more than just a physical form; it represents a sacred embodiment of the divine that aids in spiritual communion and worship.

Ichnographically, Dakṣiṇāmūrti is depicted as a form of Shiva seated under a banyan tree, facing the south (hence the name), and teaching in silence to the sages who sit before him. This silent teaching represents the highest form of imparting knowledge, suggesting that the deepest truths are beyond words and are grasped only in deep contemplation.

Furthermore, the southward orientation has symbolic significance. In Vedanta cosmology, the south direction is often associated with the realm of death and change, overseen by the deity Yama (God of death). By facing south, Dakṣiṇāmūrti, as the eternal teacher, dispels the fear of death and change, and bestows knowledge that leads to immortality and eternal truth.

It difficult to pinpoint the exact origin or the first utterance of the name "Dakṣiṇāmūrti." It's likely that the concept and reverence for this form of Shiva evolved organically over time within the Shaiva tradition, and its earliest mentions could be found in ancient texts, hymns, and scriptures.

One of the most notable elaborations on the philosophy and significance of Dakṣiṇāmūrti is found in this Dakṣiṇāmūrti Stotram, attributed to Adi Shankaracharya. Adi Shankaracharya was a pivotal figure in reviving and consolidating Advaita Vedanta philosophy, and his hymns and writings have had a significant influence on the development of modern Vedanta thought. Whether he was the first to utter the name or simply a significant proponent is not clear, but his association with the Dakṣiṇāmūrti Stotram has firmly established the importance of this aspect of Shiva in the Vedanta tradition.

Adi Shankaracharya belonging to the early 8th century traveled extensively across the Indian sub-continent, visiting important pilgrimage sites, debating scholars, and establishing monastic centers (mathas). Given this extensive travel, it's challenging to pinpoint the exact location where he might have composed any specific work unless it's explicitly mentioned in traditional biographies or other texts.

What is a Stotram?

A Stotram is a song of praise dedicated to a deity, saint, or sacred object. They are often recited as acts of devotion and can be found in various lengths, from short to very long. For example, the "Lalita Sahasranama" is a Stotram dedicated to the goddess Lalita, where she is praised through a thousand names.

The term स्तोत्रम् (Stotram) is derived from the root verb स्तु (stu), which means "to praise" or "to eulogize." From this root, we get the verb स्तौति (stauti), which means "he/she praises." The noun form derived from this verb is स्तोत्र (Stotra), which refers to a song of praise.

While "sotram" is often translated as "hymn," the nuances between the two are distinct and noteworthy. The term "hymn" predominantly refers to a religious song or poem in Western religious traditions, usually in praise of God. Contrastingly, many Stotrams are also rich in philosophical concepts. They aren't just songs of praise; they deeply imbue the spiritual and philosophical teachings of their originating tradition. Within Stotrams, one finds discussions on cosmology and creation, where some describe the genesis of the universe, the roles of various deities, and the dynamic of cosmic principles. Such descriptions guide devotees in understanding their position within the vast cosmos.

Furthermore, the nature of the divine is a frequent theme in Stotrams. They shed light on attributes of the divine, whether it represents the formless Brahman or a deity with specific traits. A quintessential example is the portrayal of Shiva in several Stotrams, where he is depicted as both a creator and a destroyer.

Additionally, Stotrams provide insights into human nature and our purpose. They contemplate the nature of the human soul, referred to as Ātman, and its intricate relationship with the divine, or Brahman. Discussions often revolve around the soul's eternal essence, its traversal through cycles of birth and death, and the aspirational goal of liberation, or Mokśa.

Guidance on the paths to this liberation is also a characteristic feature of Stotrams. They might advocate for particular spiritual practices or paths, such as Bhakti-Yoga or Jnana-Yoga, to fortify a bond with the divine or to attain liberation. Beyond the spiritual, Stotrams offer moral and ethical direction. Through their verses, they emphasize righteous living, the significance of virtues, and the repercussions of vice.

Some Stotrams even venture into the exploration of reality, drawing distinctions between the illusory nature of the material world, termed Māya, and the ultimate reality, known as Brahman or ParamĀtman. A poignant example of such philosophical depth is the "Nirvāna śatakam," attributed to Adi Shankaracharya. This Stotram resonates with the philosophy of non-dualism, or Advaita Vedanta, where it highlights the genuine nature of the self by negating identifications with transient entities like the body or emotions, and affirming an identity with the boundless consciousness.

While Stotrams may primarily resonate as devotional compositions, they act as vessels conveying profound philosophical truths. This dual role makes them invaluable for those pursuing both spiritual devotion and philosophical understanding.

The Dakṣiṇāmūrti Stotram stands out among other stotras due to its profound philosophical content, the unique nature of the deity it venerates, and its emphasis on silent transmission of knowledge. It's not just a hymn of praise but a guide to understanding the deeper truths of existence.

Chapter 2

Significance of Dakshimamurthi Stotram

The Dakṣiṇāmūrti aspect of Shiva symbolizes the ultimate teacher of yoga, wisdom, and knowledge. It emphasizes the importance of contemplation, and the inner guru or self.

While the Vedas contain hymns dedicated to Rudra (a form of Shiva), the specific concept of Dakṣiṇāmūrti is not explicitly mentioned in the Vedas. However, the philosophical underpinnings that inform the concept of Dakṣiṇāmūrti, such as the knowledge of the self, cosmic truths, meditation, and the relationship between the teacher and the student, have Vedic origins and can be found in texts like the Upanishads. For a detailed exposition on Dakṣiṇāmūrti, one would typically turn to later texts, including the Puranas, the āgamās (canonical texts), and various scriptures and hymns dedicated specifically to Lord Shiva.

The main symbolisms associated with Guru Dakṣiṇāmūrti are as follows:

Metaphors in the Stotram

* Under the Banyan Tree: Dakṣiṇāmūrti is depicted seated under a banyan tree. This tree symbolizes time and the vast expanse of the universe. The aerial roots of the banyan signify the endless descent of knowledge from the divine to the material realm.

* Chinmudra: The gesture formed by his fingers – thumb and forefinger touching each other while the other three fingers are extended – symbolizes the unity of the individual soul with the ultimate soul (Brahman). The three extended fingers represent the three states of consciousness: waking, dreaming, and deep sleep. The silent impartation of this wisdom, via the mudra, reinforces the idea that such profound truths are best conveyed in stillness.

* Youthful Form: Despite being the embodiment of supreme wisdom, Dakṣiṇāmūrti is shown as a youthful deity. This represents the timeless and eternal nature of truth and knowledge.

* Fire and Fuel: The relationship between Brahman and the universe is likened to that of fire and its fuel. Just as fuel, when burnt, becomes indistinguishable from the fire, the universe, in its true essence, is non-different from Brahman.

- Ocean and Waves: The waves in an ocean are nothing but the ocean itself. Similarly, the manifold universe is nothing but manifestations of the singular Brahman.
- Space in a Pot: Just as space inside a pot is no different from the space outside it, the individual soul, limited by the body (the pot), is essentially the same as the ultimate soul.

Cultural Significance

- Guru-Shishya Tradition: Dakṣiṇāmūrti, seated beneath a tree with disciples at his feet, embodies the ancient guru-shishya (teacher-student) tradition. This image emphasizes the reverence Vedantas have for the teacher or guru as the one who dispels darkness and brings light to the mind.
- Art and Architecture: Temples dedicated to Shiva often have a niche on the southern wall depicting Dakṣiṇāmūrti as a teacher. In the realm of dance and sculpture, his form has been depicted and celebrated, symbolizing the dance of creation and dissolution.
- Guru Purnima Celebrations: Guru Purnima, a day dedicated to honoring spiritual and academic teachers, is celebrated with great fervor. Devotees and students might recite the Dakṣiṇāmūrti Stotram on this day as a mark of respect and gratitude to their gurus.

Dream Analogy

The Stotram often uses the analogy of a dream to explain Māya. In a dream, we experience a reality with its events, emotions, and consequences. However, upon waking, we realize the dream's fleeting nature. Similarly, the universe, with its myriad of experiences, is likened to a dream when compared to the absolute reality of Brahman.

The dream analogy used in the Dakṣiṇāmūrti Stotram is a profound metaphor to convey the Advaita Vedanta philosophy and the nature of reality. In this analogy, Adi Shankaracharya likens the waking state, dream state, and deep sleep state to different levels of reality.

1. Waking State (Jāgrat): This state is compared to the waking world, where we perceive and interact with the external physical reality. In this state, we experience duality, where there is a distinction between the subject (the individual consciousness) and the object (the external world).

2. Dream State (Swapna): The dream state is likened to the experiences that occur in our dreams. Just as dreams seem real while we are asleep, our waking experiences also seem real when we are in the waking state. In both states, there is a sense of duality, where the dreamer or the experiencer perceives a multiplicity of objects and events.

3. Deep Sleep State (Suśupti): The deep sleep state is described as a state of profound rest and bliss, where there is no awareness of the external world or even the dream world. It is a state of undifferentiated consciousness, where the boundaries between subject and object dissolve.

The key message of this analogy is that just as we realize the unreality of dream experiences when we wake up, similarly, one can attain enlightenment by realizing the unreality of the waking state. In Advaita Vedanta, the ultimate truth is the non-dual consciousness (Brahman), which is beyond all distinctions and is the substratum of all states of consciousness.

Cosmic Teacher (Guru)

Sri Dakṣiṇāmūrti is symbolic of the universal teacher. The silence of Dakṣiṇāmūrti is the highest form of teaching, revealing the profound truths of existence beyond words.

Sri Dakṣiṇāmūrti is not just any guru; He represents the culmination of all wisdom and knowledge. His presence embodies the supreme truths of the universe. In the Indian tradition, the Guru is often revered as one who dispels ignorance (darkness) and bestows knowledge (light). Sri Dakṣiṇāmūrti does this not by verbal teachings alone but through His very essence.

Traditional teaching often involves a transfer of knowledge through words, books, or other mediums. However, Dakṣiṇāmūrti 's teachings transcend these conventional means. His silent presence imparts knowledge, reminding us that true wisdom often lies beyond the surface, awaiting silent contemplation and introspection to be unearthed. His silence is profound and filled with meaning. In the world of spirituality, there's an understanding that the deepest truths cannot be conveyed through words alone. Words can be misinterpreted, but direct experience is unambiguous. The silence of Dakṣiṇāmūrti is akin to this direct experience, providing an unmediated understanding of the truth.

To grasp the teachings of Dakṣiṇāmūrti, one doesn't merely listen or read; one meditates. His silent form encourages seekers to turn inward and meditate on the Self. This inner journey, facilitated by the meditative presence of Dakṣiṇāmūrti, leads to self-realization and an experiential understanding of His teachings.

The iconography associated with Dakṣiṇāmūrti further reinforces His role as the Cosmic Teacher. Seated under a banyan tree, He is surrounded by sages and scholars, symbolizing the eternal tradition of knowledge transfer. His foot often rests on a demon, symbolizing ignorance being subdued. The banyan tree itself, with its vast spread and deep roots, signifies the vastness of knowledge and its profound depths.

In essence, Sri Dakṣiṇāmūrti as the Cosmic Teacher emphasizes the idea that the ultimate truths of existence are often beyond verbal articulation. True wisdom and understanding arise from direct experience, contemplation, and introspection, guided by the silent presence of the Guru.

Through rich metaphors and symbolism, it communicates the intricate philosophy of non-dualism, emphasizing the role of the Guru in guiding seekers toward this profound realization.

Youth and Elders

In the iconic imagery, Dakṣiṇāmūrti is depicted as a young teacher seated under a banyan tree, surrounded by elderly sages. This represents the timeless wisdom of the self that doesn't age, even as the body undergoes change.

Sri Dakṣiṇāmūrti, being depicted as a young divine figure, symbolizes the eternal nature of wisdom. Youth is often associated with vigor, freshness, and immutability. By presenting the divine teacher in youthful form, the Stotram underscores the idea that true knowledge and wisdom are timeless, remaining unaltered through the ages.

Surrounding the young Dakṣiṇāmūrti are the aged sages, seeking wisdom. The elderly form of the disciples portrays the transience of human life and the inevitable progression of age. Despite their advanced years and accumulated experiences, these sages sit at the feet of the youthful Dakṣiṇāmūrti, emphasizing that while the body ages, the quest for knowledge and the soul's wisdom remain perennial.

The juxtaposition of the young guru and old disciples offers a profound message. It suggests that true wisdom is not merely a factor of age or experience. While the sages bring with them a lifetime of experiences, it is at the feet of this eternal youth that they find the deepest truths.

No matter one's age, the pursuit of truth and understanding is a constant journey. The elderly sages, despite their vast life experiences, display a humble acknowledgment that the deeper mysteries of existence are yet to be fully grasped, and they can be understood from the eternal youth, Dakṣiṇāmūrti.

The portrayal also speaks of the cyclical nature of life and knowledge. The young and the old are but stages in the endless cycle of existence. Knowledge, symbolized by the youthful Dakṣiṇāmūrti, remains a constant amidst this cycle, unchanging and ever-relevant.

The imagery of revered elderly sages sitting at the feet of a young guru underscores the virtue of humility in the path of learning. True seekers of knowledge acknowledge that wisdom can come from the most unexpected sources, and age is not always the determinant of depth in understanding.

In summary, the theme of Youth and Elders in the Dakṣiṇāmūrti Stotram serves as a powerful allegory. It drives home the message that wisdom is eternal and unchanging, whereas the human experience, represented by the aged sages, is transient. The ever-youthful Sri Dakṣiṇāmūrti stands as a beacon of timeless knowledge and truth, guiding souls through the transient phases of life.

Chapter 3

PHILOSOPHICAL EXPLORATION

The unchanging background

The Dakṣiṇāmūrti Stotram is a poetic exposition of the principles of Advaita Vedanta. It delves into the nature of reality, the illusion of duality, and the transcendental knowledge that dispels this illusion.

Advaita Vedanta is referred to as a "darshana" which offers a philosophical framework for examining profound questions about the self and the world. The root of the Sanskrit word दर्शन (darshana) is दृश् (drish), which means "to see" or "to perceive." In the context of Vedanta and other Indian philosophical traditions, darshana refers to the philosophical and spiritual perspective or viewpoint through which one perceives and understands the world, reality, and the self.

At the core of Advaita Vedanta is the principle of unchanging reality and asserts that *any change presupposes an unchanging background.* Central to this philosophy is its emphasis on the perpetual, immutable truth (Brahman) as the foundation of the dynamic, ever-changing world (jagat). Even as the world around us undergoes continuous transformations, from birth to decay, there's a steadfast reality underpinning these shifts. This unchanging background is given the name, Brahman, whereas the changing world is referred to as jagat.

The term Brahman is derived from the Sanskrit root बृह् (bṛh), which means "to grow" or "to expand." The etymological roots of Brahman suggest a concept related to vastness and infinite expansion. It points to something that is beyond the ordinary, limited, and finite aspects of existence. Brahman signifies the underlying essence that is beyond expression, time, space, and causality.

The concept of "jagat" represents the physical world or the material contents of the universe. The term jagat is derived from the root गम् (gam) or गच्छ (gacch), which means "to go" or "to move." Jagat is often described as, गच्छति इति जगत् (gachati it jagat). It essentially conveys the idea of that which is constantly moving or changing, referring to the dynamic nature of the world.

Jagat can also be referred to as Prakruti (प्रकृति) which can be broken down into prakṛṣṭam (प्रकृष्टम्) and kṛtiḥ (कृति:). Here, the prefix "pra" (प्र) signifies emphasis, excellence, or the original state. Prakṛṣṭam can be understood as the supreme or excellent state or condition. Krithihi is derived from the root "kru" (कृ) in Sanskrit, which means "to do." Kṛtiḥ can be more accurately translated as action or manifestation. Jagat or Prakruti means, the phenomenal world that is of the nature of intense activity or change.

Jagat in Vedantic philosophy represents not only the contents of the world but also the dimensions of time and space.

- **Physical World with its Contents (Dravya)**: Jagat includes the tangible and intangible aspects of the physical world. This encompasses all living beings, objects, substances, and phenomena that exist in the universe. It refers to the diversity of forms and entities that constitute the observable and experiential realm.

- **Space (Deśa)**: Jagat extends to the spatial dimension, encompassing the physical space in which all things exist and interact. It includes the vastness of the cosmos, the physical environment of the Earth, and the spatial relationships among objects and entities within the universe.

- **Time (Kāla)**: Jagat also includes the dimension of time. This encompasses the past, present, and future, as well as the continuous flow of events and changes that occur within the universe. Time is an integral part of the dynamic and ever-changing nature of jagat.

- **Qualities (Gunas):** The interplay of three "gunas" is believed to govern the characteristics and attributes of all things within jagat. Gunas refer to the three fundamental qualities or attributes—sattva (purity and balance), rajas (activity and passion), and tamas (inertia and ignorance)—which are inherently present within the material and mental universe, shape and govern the characteristics and behavior of all things. These qualities, in varying degrees, influence the nature and dynamics of jagat, including individuals, objects, and abstract concepts.

- **Dynamic and Interconnected Nature:** The concept of jagat emphasizes the dynamic and interconnected nature of the universe. It recognizes that everything within the world is in a constant state of flux and change, and that the interactions between time, space, and the contents of the world shape the experiences and evolution of all entities.

- **Spiritual and Philosophical Significance:** Understanding jagat in this comprehensive way has spiritual and philosophical significance. It highlights the impermanence and transience of all things, including time and space, and underscores the idea that attachment to the ever-changing aspects of the world can lead to suffering. Many spiritual paths advocate transcending the limitations of jagat to seek a deeper, timeless reality or spiritual truth beyond the physical, temporal, and spatial dimensions.

However, for us to recognize and understand the changes in jagat, there must be an unchanging and immutable reference point, which according to Advaita Vedanta, is the Brahman. Within each of us is the awareness that is the witness to the changing world.

This Advaita Vedanta proposition can be logically deduced. Consider the analogy of a movie projected onto a screen. The scenes, characters, and events in the movie are ever-changing, much like the phenomena in jagat. But for the movie to be visible, there needs to be a stable screen onto which it is projected. This screen, which remains unchanged regardless of the movie's content, can be likened to Brahman.

Certain Buddhist doctrines emphasize the concept of "anicca" or impermanence, suggesting that everything, without exception, is in a state of flux but there's no permanent entity or background; everything is interdependent. However, to grasp the significance of the Advaita Vedantic postulation, *any change presupposes an unchanging background*, we require some foundational knowledge of the transient world and the unchanging background.

1. **Impermanence**: Impermanence is a fundamental characteristic of the world around us. Flowers bloom and wither, civilizations rise and fall, and

rivers change their courses. However, for us to recognize these changes, there must be some constants. For instance, the life cycle of a flower is observed against the constant backdrop of time. A train moves along a fixed track. An airplane in flight undergoes various changes – it accelerates, decelerates, ascends, and descends. Yet, all these changes occur within the vast expanse of the unchanging sky.

2.   **Frames of Reference**: In physics, especially when discussing motion, a frame of reference is essential. This frame, whether it's the ground for a running animal or the stationary stars for a rotating Earth, provides a constant against which changes (or motions) are measured. Even in Einstein's relativity, where there's no absolute frame, the speed of light remains a constant, serving as an unchanging backdrop against which relative motions are understood.

3.   **Perception and Cognition**: On a cognitive level, our minds rely on constants to detect and make sense of changes. For instance, we recognize the changing seasons against the constant cycle of a year. Our perception is anchored in certain unchanging principles or backgrounds, which allow us to discern variations.

4.   **Beyond Our Universe**: Even when speculating about realms beyond our universe, the concept

holds. If there were multiple universes with different laws of physics (as in the multiverse hypothesis), the very framework or theory that proposes the multiverse becomes the unchanging backdrop against which the differences between these universes are understood.

In essence, the statement (*any change presupposes an unchanging background*) underscores a foundational idea in both philosophy and science: change, in its myriad forms, is discernible and meaningful only when contrasted with something constant or unchanging. This unchanging background, whether it's a philosophical absolute, a physical constant, or a perceptual anchor, provides context and depth to our understanding of change.

Understanding Consciousness

From childhood to adulthood, through middle age, and into old age, our bodies undergo constant change. Yet, amidst this transformation, there is a constant within us – the essence of self, which is "I am." We sense that the "I" that observes our body and mind evolving over time remains unaltered. We intuitively recognize an enduring awareness that witnesses the shifts in our physical form.

In Advaita Vedanta philosophy, the term used to describe individual awareness is "Ātman."

Ātman represents the individual self and serves as the core of one's consciousness. Moreover, Advaita Vedanta further posits that the true nature of the individual self (Ātman) is identical to the universal consciousness (Brahman).

Consciousness is a profound and multifaceted phenomenon that has intrigued philosophers, scientists, and seekers of truth for centuries. It is approached and understood differently from two distinct but complementary perspectives: the Vedantic standpoint and the standpoint of neuro science.

Vedantic Consciousness

The term "consciousness" is often used as a translation for "Brahman," but it is an inadequate translation that falls short of conveying the deeper meaning.

The Sanskrit term often used to refer to Vedantic consciousness or Brahman is चैतन्य (Chaitanya). In Advaita Vedanta, Chaitanya is considered the fundamental essence of reality. It encompasses both individual consciousness (Ātman) and universal consciousness (Brahman). Chaitanya is often described as non-dual, eternal, and all-pervading.

Advaita Vedanta operates within a framework that is different from the naturalistic perspective of Western philosophy and science. It posits a fundamental distinction between the physical world and the metaphysical reality of consciousness (Chaitanya/Brahman).

Contemporary scholars and translators have used the term "consciousness" as one way to convey the Chaitanya to English-speaking readers, but it's not a direct one-to-one translation. From the Vedantic perspective, Chaitanya is not merely a product of the physical brain or a byproduct of biological processes. Instead, it is considered the unchanging and eternal substratum of existence itself. Vedanta posits that Chaitanya is the ultimate reality, the source from which the entire universe emanates, and the essence of everything in creation. It is limitless, unbounded, and transcendent, existing beyond the limitations of time and space.

According to Vedanta, the fundamental human problem is the failure to recognize this intrinsic oneness of the Ātman with the Brahman. Through practices like meditation, self-inquiry, and the study of scriptures, individuals can realize their true nature as pure consciousness. This realization is often described as the highest form of knowledge, leading to liberation or "mokśa" from the cycle of birth and death, known as "samsāra."

In the Vedantic view, Chaitanya is not confined to the individual self but is the very essence of the entire existence. It is the source of all knowledge, existence, and bliss, and it underlies all subjective and objective experiences. Vedanta's perspective on Chaitanya transcends the physical and material realm, offering a profound understanding of the nature of reality itself.

Neuroscientific Consciousness

From the standpoint of Western philosophy and neuroscience, consciousness is approached in a fundamentally different manner. Here, consciousness is an epiphenomenon of the brain and its complex neural networks. While science has made remarkable progress in understanding the neural correlates of consciousness, it still grapples with questions about the precise nature and origin of consciousness.

Neuroscience views consciousness as a product of the brain's intricate electrochemical processes. It considers the brain as the physical substrate that gives rise to subjective experience, self-awareness, and perception of the external world. Studies in neuroscience have identified specific brain regions and activities associated with different aspects of consciousness, such as sensory perception, memory, and higher-order cognitive functions.

States of consciousness, including waking, dreaming, and deep sleep, have been extensively studied within the neuroscience field. Researchers use various tools, including electroencephalography (EEG) and functional magnetic resonance imaging (fMRI), to investigate how different brain states correspond to different subjective experiences.

Altered states of consciousness, induced by factors like anesthesia, meditation, or psychoactive substances, are also subjects of scientific investigation. These altered states challenge the traditional understanding of consciousness and offer insights into the brain's flexibility and adaptability.

Despite significant progress, the neuroscience perspective on consciousness remains a subject of ongoing research and debate. The "hard problem of consciousness" is a term coined by philosopher David Chalmers. It refers to the difficulty of explaining how and why physical processes in the brain give rise to subjective, first-person conscious experiences. In other words, it's the challenge of understanding why certain patterns of neural activity result in the vivid and rich qualities of conscious perception, such as the taste of chocolate or the color red.

This problem primarily centers on the subjective, qualitative, and phenomenal aspects of consciousness—the "what it's like" to have an experience. It raises questions about why certain physical processes are accompanied by subjective feelings or "qualia." The hard problem is often discussed within a naturalistic or materialistic framework, where consciousness is considered an emergent property of physical processes. It seeks to explain how the brain, which consists of neurons and synapses, can give rise to subjective conscious experiences.

The Witnessing Self

Understanding the inner self, often referred to as the observer, presents a unique challenge. While it's possible to perceive oneself as distinct from the contents of the mind—such as feelings, thoughts, emotions, and fears—attempting to isolate and grasp the witnessing self can give rise to a logical fallacy recognized in Western philosophy as the "fallacy of misplaced concreteness" or the "reification fallacy." This fallacy occurs when an abstract concept or mental construct is erroneously treated as if it possessed concrete, tangible qualities.

In Advaita Vedanta, the "witnessing self" or Chaitanya represents the awareness that observes thoughts, sensations, and experiences but is itself formless and devoid of specific attributes. Unlike physical objects that can be perceived through the senses and grasped as concrete entities, consciousness lacks tangibility. It cannot be seen, touched, heard, smelled, or tasted in the same way that physical objects can.

The witnessing self is paradoxical in that it is both intimately known to us as the essence of our awareness and yet elusive when we try to objectify or isolate it. This paradox underscores the limitations of trying to grasp consciousness as if it were a concrete object.

Our attempts to isolate and grasp the witnessing self often fail because consciousness is not something separate from our subjective experience; it is the very essence of our subjective experience. It's like trying to see the eye with the eye or trying to bite one's own teeth.

The fallacy arises when one attempts to treat the witnessing self as if it were an object of observation. In reality, the witnessing self is the subject—the one doing the observing—rather than an object that can be observed. It is the process of awareness itself.

Consciousness Vs Chaitanya

Vedanta's consciousness (Chaitanya) is not same as the sum total of mental processes (which are emergent properties of brain). Instead, it is the illuminator or witness of all mental activities. In other words, Chaitanya is considered the illuminator of the mind and the source of all experiences. It enables the mind to function and be aware of its own activities. This relationship can be likened to a lamp illuminating a room. The lamp represents Chaitanya, while the room symbolizes the mind. The lamp's light allows you to see and experience everything within the room, but the light itself is distinct from the objects it illuminates.

Vedanta emphasizes that Chaitanya is the source of subjective experience. It is what makes thoughts, emotions, and perceptions meaningful and knowable. Without Chaitanya, the mind's activities would be devoid of awareness and significance. It's important to note that Vedanta holds that Chaitanya is not limited or confined by the brain or the mind. Instead, it transcends them and is unchanging and eternal.

Consciousness within Western philosophy and science focuses on the relationship between physical processes and subjective experience. In contrast, Chaitanya in Advaita Vedanta is a concept that delves into the nature of consciousness as the ultimate reality and the path to self-realization and spiritual liberation. They may touch upon similar themes, but they have distinct objectives.

The Oneness of Ātman and Brahman

As mentioned earlier, the realization that Ātman and Brahman are one and the same is the ultimate goal in Advaita Vedanta, leading to liberation (mokśa) from the cycle of birth and rebirth.

The phrase "Brahma satyam jagat mithyā, Jīvo Brahmaiva nāparah" is often cited as a summary or encapsulation of the teachings of Advaita Vedanta. This verse is found in "Brahmajnanavalimala," a work attributed to Adi Shankaracharya. ब्रह्म (Brahma)–ज्ञान (jñāna)–आवलि (āvali)–माला (māla), when combined, "Brahmajnanavalimala" can be translated as "a garland (or series) of knowledge about Brahman" or "A string of verses on the knowledge of the ultimate reality." It's a concise work that encapsulates the teachings of Advaita Vedanta, providing insights into the nature of Brahman, the self, and the relationship between the individual soul (Jīva) and the ultimate reality.

ब्रह्म सत्यं जगन्मिथ्या जीवो ब्रह्मैव नापरः ।

अनेन वेद्यं सच्छास्त्रमिति वेदान्तडिण्डिमः ॥ २०॥

Brahma satyam jaganmithyā jīvo brahmaiva nāparaḥ I

anena vedyam sacchāstram iti vedāntaḍiṇḍimaḥ II 20 II

Translation and Explanation

* ब्रह्म सत्यं (Brahma Satyam): Brahman is the truth. This means that the ultimate reality or the absolute truth is Brahman, which is eternal and unchanging.

* जगन्मिथ्या (Jaganmithya): The world is an illusion. This suggests that the world, as we perceive it, is unreal. It's transient and ever-changing, unlike Brahman which is constant.

* जीवो ब्रह्मैव नापरः (Jivo Brahmaiva Na Aparah): The individual soul (Jīva) is none other than Brahman itself. This emphasizes the non-dual nature of Advaita Vedanta, suggesting that the individual soul, when stripped of ignorance, realizes its true nature as Brahman.

* अनेन वेद्यं (Anena Vedyam): By this (knowledge or realization).

* सच्छास्त्रमिति (Sacchastramiti) is broken down to सत् शास्त्रम् इति (Sat Shastram Iti): The true scripture or the true teaching is.

* वेदान्तडिण्डिमः (Vedanta-Dindimah): The declaration or proclamation of Vedanta.

When combined, the verse can be translated as:

Brahman is the truth, the world is an illusion, and the individual soul is none other than Brahman itself. By this knowledge, the true teaching is declared in Vedanta.

This verse succinctly encapsulates the core teachings of Advaita Vedanta, emphasizing the non-dual nature of the self and the ultimate reality, the illusory nature of the world, and the essence of the teachings of Vedanta.

Ātman and Jīva Explained

In Vedanta, the concepts of "Ātman" and "Jīva" are often used to discuss the nature of the self and the individual soul. Their relationship can be understood in the context of the broader cosmology and the quest for self-realization.

Ātman is roughly translated as "self" or "soul." In the Upanishads, the Ātman is often described as the ultimate, unchanging reality behind the universe. It is pure consciousness, eternal, and is often equated with Brahman, the absolute reality or universal soul. In this context, the Ātman is the universal Self present in every being.

The Jīva is the individualized soul that is born into the physical world, goes through various experiences, and is subject to the laws of karma and the cycle of birth and death (samsāra). The term Jīva is sometimes translated as "individual soul." The Jīva is essentially the Ātman associated with a body and mind, entangled in the material world due to ignorance (avidya) of its true nature.

The relationship between Ātman and Jīva, in the context of Advaita Vedanta philosophy, can be understood through the analogy of electricity and a light bulb. Ātman represents the universal, indivisible, and eternal essence of consciousness. It is akin to the electricity that powers all electrical devices in a house. Ātman is beyond individuality and is the same in every living being and in the entire universe. In the analogy, Ātman is like the electricity that flows through all the devices in a house, providing the energy for their functions. It is the source from which everything arises and returns.

Jīva, on the other hand, represents the individual self or the embodied soul. It is comparable to a specific electrical device, such as a light bulb, which operates using the electricity (Ātman) but has its unique characteristics. Jīva is the individualized consciousness that experiences life, thoughts, and emotions within the physical body. Each living being has its own Jīva, distinct in its experiences and karma.

Imagine a light bulb as the Jīva and electricity as the Ātman. The light bulb can only function and emit light when it is connected to the electricity source. Similarly, the Jīva can only experience life and consciousness when connected to the universal Ātman.

Just as multiple light bulbs can be connected to the same electrical source, numerous Jīvas are connected to the same universal Ātman. Each light bulb shines with its unique brightness and characteristics, similar to how each Jīva has its own individuality and experiences.

Despite the apparent individuality of the light bulbs and the devices they power, the source of electricity is singular and undivided. Likewise, in Vedanta, the individual Jīvas may seem distinct, but they all arise from and are ultimately connected to the universal Ātman.

The key insight here is that, just as the electricity remains unchanged while powering various devices, the universal Ātman remains unchanged while manifesting as individual Jīvas. This highlights the profound Vedantic principle of unity and oneness in the midst of apparent diversity.

Indivisibility of Ātman and Jīva

At the deepest level, there is no distinction between Ātman and Jīva. The Ātman is the core essence of every Jīva. The difference arises only due to the layers of ignorance, ego, and material entanglement that cover the true nature of the Jīva. In this sense, every individual soul (Jīva) is essentially the universal Self (Ātman) in its core.

The primary ignorance (avidya) is the mistaken identification of the self with the body, mind, and ego. Due to this, the Jīva feels separated from the universal consciousness and undergoes the cycle of births and deaths. The primary goal of many spiritual paths in Hinduism is to realize the true nature of the Jīva as the Ātman, leading to liberation (mokśa) from the cycle of samsāra.

Several metaphors in the Upanishads elucidate this relationship. One of the most famous is the two birds on the same tree from the Mundaka Upanishad, third khanda (section) of the first Mundaka.

द्वा सुपर्णा सयुजा सखाया समानं वृक्षं परिषस्वजाते।
तयोरन्यः पिप्पलं स्वाद्वत्त्यनश्नन्नन्यो अभिचाकशीति।।

dvā suparṇā sayujā sakhāyā samānaṃ vṛkṣaṃ
pariṣasvajāte|

tayoranyaḥ pippalaṃ svādvattyanaśnannanyo
abhicākaśīti||

Meaning

द्वा (dvā) – Two; सुपर्णा (suparṇā) - Having beautiful wings; here it refers to birds; सयुजा (sayujā) - United, conjoined; सखाया (sakhāyā) - Friends, companions; समानं (samānaṃ) - Same, identical; वृक्षं (vṛkṣaṃ) – Tree; परिषस्वजाते (pariṣasvajāte) - (They) cling to, perch on; तयोः (tayoḥ) - Of the two; अन्यः (anyaḥ) – other; पिप्पलं (pippalaṃ) - Fig; here it can be interpreted as the fruit of the tree; स्वादु (svādu) - Sweet, tasty; अत्ति (atti) – Eats; अनश्नन् (anaśnan) - Without eating, not eating; अन्यो (anyo) - The other; अभिचाकशीति (abhicākaśīti) - Simply looks on, observes.

Translation

Two birds, united always and known as friends, cling to the same tree.

Of these, one eats the sweet fruit of the tree, but the other simply looks on without eating.

This verse beautifully encapsulates the relationship between the jīva (individual soul) and the paramātman (universal soul or supreme Self) within each of us, using the allegory of the two birds. One bird (representing the Jīva) hops around eating the fruit, while the other bird (representing the Ātman) merely watches without eating. The first bird represents the individual soul engrossed in worldly experiences, while the second represents the undisturbed, eternal self.

In many Hindu philosophical schools, the ultimate goal of human life is to recognize and experience the oneness of Jīva and Ātman, realizing that one's true nature is not the limited individual self but the infinite, universal Self.

The path to Self-Realization is primarily an inward journey. While the external world offers myriad experiences, it is by turning one's attention inward, towards the inner self, that the profound truths are realized. Sri Dakṣiṇāmūrti, with his meditative pose, exemplifies this introspection, urging seekers to delve within.

Self-Realization is not just an intellectual acknowledgment of a concept. It's an experiential recognition that permeates one's entire being. It's akin to the difference between knowing about honey and actually tasting it. Sri Dakṣiṇāmūrti 's teachings guide aspirants from mere theoretical knowledge to a direct experience of the Self.

A significant barrier to Self-Realization is the ego or the sense of individual identity. This ego creates a sense of separation from the rest of existence. As one progresses on the path of Self-Realization, the ego is transcended, paving the way for the experience of oneness.

Self-Realization also marks the end of dualities. The dichotomies of joy and sorrow, pain and pleasure, birth and death, all merge into a unified experience. The realized individual sees the same divine principle in everything, transcending the boundaries of conventional dualistic perception.

Achieving Self-Realization is Mokśa or liberation. Mokśa is freedom from the cycle of birth and death and the associated sufferings. With the realization of the true nature of the self, one is no longer bound by the karmic cycle and attains eternal peace and bliss.

While self-effort is crucial, the grace of the Guru (in this context, Sri Dakṣiṇāmūrti) plays an indispensable role in Self Realization. The Guru acts as a mirror, reflecting the disciple's true nature back to them. The silent teachings of Dakṣiṇāmūrti act as a catalyst, hastening the aspirant's journey towards realizing their true essence.

In the Dakṣiṇāmūrti Stotram, Self-Realization is portrayed as the pinnacle of spiritual aspiration. Sri Dakṣiṇāmūrti , as the cosmic teacher, guides seekers on this profound journey, helping them transcend barriers, dispel illusions, and ultimately recognize their innate divine nature.

Cause and Effect

Advaita Vedanta's perspective on cause-effect relationship is understood in the context of the ultimate reality (Brahman) and the manifest world (Jagat). Here's how Advaita Vedanta explains this relationship:

Satkārya Vāda (Theory of Pre-existence of the Effect): Advaita Vedanta subscribes to the Satkārya Vāda doctrine, which posits that the effect (kārya) already exists in its cause (kāraṇa) in a potential form before its manifestation. According to Satkārya Vāda, causality is not a process of creating something new but rather a process of unveiling or bringing forth what already exists in potential. For instance, a pot (effect) exists in a lump of clay (cause) before it's shaped. According to this theory, the pot pre-exists in the form of the clay; it is just a transformation of the clay.

Satkārya Vāda highlights that the ultimate reality, Brahman, is always present and that the process of realizing one's true nature involves recognizing the inherent non-dual nature of existence and transcending the illusory world of cause and effect.

Vivarta Vāda (Theory of Apparent Modification): The world's manifestation from Brahman is described as Vivarta, meaning apparent or seeming transformation. According to this theory, Brahman, the ultimate reality, appears as the world without undergoing any real change. This is analogous to how a rope might be mistakenly perceived as a snake in dim light. The rope hasn't transformed into a snake; it only appears so. In this analogy, the rope represents the unchanging Brahman, and the mistaken perception of a snake symbolizes the world of appearances created by Māya.

Vivarta Vāda distinguishes between transformation (vivarta) and modification (pariṇāma). While modification implies a real change in the nature of something, transformation in this context suggests that the change is only apparent. The world appears to change, but its fundamental reality remains Brahman.

Central to Vivarta Vāda is the concept of Māya, which is the power of illusion or delusion. Māya veils the true nature of Brahman and creates the appearance of a diverse and changing world, including all physical objects, living beings, and experiences.

Brahman as Both Material and Efficient Cause: Brahman is seen as both the "Upādāna kāraṇa" (material cause) and "Nimitta Kāraṇa" (efficient cause) of the universe.

An "efficient cause" refers to the primary or initiating cause that brings about an effect or change. It's the agent or force responsible for producing a particular outcome. In philosophical terms, the efficient cause is the entity or event that directly instigates or triggers the process leading to a result. For example, in the context of a sculpted statue, the sculptor, who carves the statue out of marble, would be considered the efficient cause, while the marble is the material cause.

According to Advaita Vedanta, Brahman is not only the substance from which the universe arises but also the force or intelligence behind its manifestation.

Mithyatva (Illusoriness of the World): The world (Jagat) is termed "mithya," which means it has a dependent reality. It's not absolutely real (like Brahman) nor absolutely unreal (like a square circle). Its reality is contingent upon Brahman. Ultimately, the cause-effect perception in the world is itself considered mithya, as it's based on the illusory appearance of the world.

Māya (Cosmic Illusion): Māya is the cosmic power that makes the one Brahman appear as many, creating the illusion of differentiation and multiplicity. It's due to Māya that the non-dual Brahman appears as the world of diverse objects, beings, and phenomena. The cause-effect relationships we perceive in the world are also due to this Māya.

Māya is often described as the "Shakti" (power or energy) of Brahman. While Brahman is the unchanging, absolute reality, Māya is the dynamic power that creates the ever-changing relative world.

For the realized person who has attained the knowledge of Brahman, the distinctions of cause-and-effect dissolve. They see everything as an expression of the non-dual Brahman. For them, the world of causality is an appearance, and the underlying reality is Brahman.

In essence, while Advaita Vedanta acknowledges the empirical reality of cause and effect in the world, it posits that, at the ultimate level, these distinctions are illusory. The true nature of reality is Brahman, which is beyond causality and differentiation.

Three levels of Reality

In the realm of Advaita Vedanta, the concepts of Pāramārthika Satyam, Prātibhāsika Satyam and Vyāvahārika Satyam are used to distinguish between different levels or orders of reality. These terms help clarify the relationship between the absolute, unchanging reality and the everyday world that we experience.

1. **Pāramārthika Satyam** (पारमार्थिक सत्यम्):

   - **Meaning**: "Pāramārthika" is derived from "parama" (supreme or ultimate) and "artha" (meaning or purpose). Thus, "pāramārthika satyam" refers to the "ultimate truth" or "absolute reality."

   - **Nature**: It is the highest order of reality, unchanging and non-dual. This level of reality pertains to Brahman, the supreme, non-dual reality behind the universe as described in Advaita Vedanta. Brahman is the substratum upon which all else is superimposed.

   - **Experience**: This truth is realized directly during moments of deep spiritual insight or enlightenment, where the distinction between the observer, the act of observing, and the observed collapses.

2. **Prātibhāsika Satyam** (प्रातिभासिक सत्यम्):

   - **Meaning:** The term " Prātibhāsika" is derived from " Pratibhāsa" (appearance or illusion), and "satyam" means "reality" or "truth." Therefore, "Prātibhāsika Satyam" signifies the "apparent reality."

   - **Nature:** Prātibhāsika Satyam represents a level of reality that is based on illusion, misperception, or subjective experience. It includes phenomena that are perceived as real by an individual but do not correspond to the ultimate or objective reality. This level of reality is characterized by the deceptive nature of appearances.

- **Experience**: Experiences within Prātibhāsika Satyam can vary widely but generally involve instances where individuals perceive something as real or valid, only to later realize that their perception was based on illusion or misperception. Common experiences that fall into this category include optical illusions, dreams, hallucinations, misperceptions, and subjective emotional reactions.

3. **Vyāvahārika Satyam** (व्यावहारिक सत्यम्):

- **Meaning**: Vyāvahārika comes from the word vyavahāra, which means "transaction" or "activity." Thus, "vyāvahārika satyam" can be understood as "transactional or the relative reality.

- **Nature**: It is the level of reality that we experience in our day-to-day lives. This reality is governed by laws of physics, time, space, causality, and duality. It's the world where there's a distinction between the self and the other, and where the laws of karma operate. Even though it's considered "real" in our daily experiences, from the standpoint of the absolute truth (pāramārthika satyam), it's considered a form of illusion or māyā. This is because it's not the ultimate reality; it's temporary and subject to change.

- **Experience**: This is the realm of everyday experiences, of waking life, and of all conventional knowledge and science.

The Relationship

- These three orders of reality help address the apparent contradiction in experiencing a world of duality and diversity while, at the same time declare the ultimate reality to be non-dual.

- The key characteristic of experiences within Prātibhāsika Satyam is that they are based on the individual's subjective perception, and what seems real or true to them may not align with the objective reality. Advaita Vedanta uses this concept to illustrate the illusory nature of the world of appearances and to emphasize the importance of discernment and realization of the ultimate truth (Pāramārthika Satyam) beyond subjective experiences.

- For a person who has realized the ultimate truth, the empirical world doesn't disappear, but its absolute reality is negated. Such a person realizes that the empirical world is a play of māyā on the substratum of Brahman. To give an analogy, think of the ocean and its waves. While waves have a relative reality (they can be seen, touched, and experienced), their absolute reality is the water of the ocean.

- This distinction also means that until one realizes the ultimate truth, one should not neglect or dismiss the empirical reality. The laws of the physical world, morality, ethics, and social responsibilities remain valid in the realm of vyāvahārika satyam.

Advaita Vedanta posits that while our empirical experiences are valid in their own domain (vyāvahārika satyam), there's a deeper, unchanging reality (pāramārthika satyam) that underlies everything, and realizing this truth is the ultimate goal of human existence.

Concept of Māya in Advaita Vedanta

One of the central tenets of Vedanta philosophy is the concept of "Māya", often translated as "illusion". This suggests that the tangible, physical world we perceive through our senses isn't the ultimate reality. Instead, it is a veil or a screen that obscures the true nature of the Self and the cosmos.

The root of the word "Māya" is derived from the Sanskrit language, and it is often associated with the idea of "mā," which means "not" or "not that." Māya is also described by the statement या मा सा माया (Yā Mā Sā Māyā)

"That which is ma (non-existent) is Māya," which suggests the idea of something that is not what it appears to be, emphasizing the illusory nature of the material world in Advaita Vedanta philosophy.

In Sanskrit grammar, the root word for "mātra" is also "मा" (mā), which means, to "measure." Some interpretations of Māyā align with this idea of measurement, portraying Māyā as that which can be quantified, while Brahman is deemed immeasurable.

Māyā is often translated as "illusion" in English, but this can be somewhat misleading. It doesn't mean that the world is not real, but rather that it is not ultimately real in the way Brahman is. The world we experience is a transient reality, constantly changing and therefore not absolute.

Māyā is described as Anirvacanīya. This means that Māyā's exact nature is challenging to define, which is where the term anirvacanīya comes into play. It means that māyā is beyond linguistic or conceptual categorization. It is neither real (because it can be sublated or negated upon the realization of Brahman) nor unreal (because it is experienced in day-to-day life). This paradoxical nature makes māyā indefinable.

The concept of अनिर्वचनीय (anirvacanīya) not only underscores the enigmatic nature of māyā but also highlights the limitations of language and human cognition. There are some truths or realities that are beyond the scope of descriptive language and can only be directly experienced or intuited.

In essence, referring to māyā as anirvacanīya captures the profound depth and mystery of the concept. It's a reminder that while philosophical discussions and intellectual pursuits are valuable, some truths in the spiritual realm are beyond intellectual grasping and can only be directly realized.

Purpose of Māya

A deeper contemplation on Māya also leads to the understanding that it isn't merely a negative or obstructive force. Instead, Māya serves a specific purpose. It facilitates the cosmic play (Lila) of creation, preservation, and dissolution. It's through the lens of Māya that the One (Brahman) appears as many.

Overcoming Māya

The ultimate goal of spiritual seekers is to transcend Māya, realizing the undifferentiated unity behind the apparent diversity. Through meditation, devotion, and the grace of the Guru (in this case, Sri Dakṣiṇāmūrti), one can see beyond the illusion to recognize the true Self.

In the Dakṣiṇāmūrti Stotram, Māya is not just a philosophical concept but a practical challenge that every spiritual aspirant must navigate. By understanding and ultimately transcending Māya, one aligns with the eternal truth, moving from the realm of illusion to the realm of true knowledge and self-realization.

Self-Realization, in this context refers to the realization of the 'Ātman' (Self) as Brahman (the ultimate reality). The Stotram suggests that true knowledge is the understanding that one's inner self is not separate from the universal consciousness.

Vedanta: A Path to Dynamic Spiritual Enlightenment

Vedanta is frequently misunderstood as advocating passivity and withdrawal from the world. Yet, a more profound exploration of Vedanta's core principles unveils a philosophy that encourages dynamic engagement with life's challenges. The same Veda that gave us Vedanta also proclaims, धर्मो रक्शति रक्शित: (dharmo rakśati rakśitaḥ) a phrase that translates to, "dharma protects those who uphold it." Dharma encompasses one's moral and ethical duties, responsibilities, and righteous conduct. Vedanta underscores the pursuit of dharma as a fundamental principle for harmonizing worldly responsibilities with the spiritual path.

Vedanta encourages individuals to fulfill their worldly responsibilities and duties with dedication and integrity. It does not endorse escapism or a renunciation of one's roles in society. Instead, it advocates that individuals engage dynamically with life's challenges, all the while recognizing the impermanence of worldly pursuits and the ultimate reality of Brahman.

Chapter 4

COMMENTARIES ON DAKṢIṆĀMŪRTI STOTRAM

Given its philosophical depth and significance, several commentaries have been written on it by various scholars to elucidate its teachings. Here are the main commentaries on the Dakṣiṇāmūrti Stotram:

1. Mānasollāsa: Sureshvara, a prominent disciple of Adi Shankaracharya, is traditionally attributed to the authorship of this vārtika (an extensive commentary) on the Dakṣiṇāmūrti Stotram. It's a detailed exposition that delves deep into the nuances of Advaita Vedanta as presented in the Stotram. While Adi Shankaracharya set the foundational principles of Advaita Vedanta, it was through the works of his direct disciples like Sureshvara that these teachings were elaborated

upon, clarified, and disseminated to a broader audience. It is a treasure trove for anyone seeking a deep and nuanced understanding of the Dakṣiṇāmūrti Stotram and Advaita Vedanta's core tenets. Sureshvara's 'Mānasollāsa' isn't a simple commentary; it's a vārtika, which means it elaborates on the Stotram verse by verse, sometimes even word by word. In this manner, Sureshvara dives deep into the meanings, extracting and elucidating nuances that may not be immediately evident to the casual reader. Noorni Ananta Krishna Sastri (1886-1964) authored a commentary on Mānasollāsa titled Mānasollāsavardhini, which serves as a valuable source for understanding the Advaita Vedanta concepts found within the Dakṣiṇāmūrti Stotram.

2. Tattvasudha by Swami Swayamprakasha Ananda (or Svayamprakashayatinindra): This is another detailed commentary that combines both rigorous philosophical discussion with elements of devotion. It explores the Stotram's teachings about the nature of Brahman, Māya, the Jīva, and their interrelations. Swami Swayamprakasha Ananda's exact dates of birth and death are not well-established, but he is generally believed to have lived during the 18th century. The work is a commentary on the Dakṣiṇāmūrti Stotram of

Adi Shankaracharya, and it stands out for its unique blend of rigorous philosophical exposition with heartfelt devotion.

3. Both these (Mānasollāsa and Tattvasudha) insightful interpretations, along with an elucidative rendition of the Dakṣiṇāmūrti Stotram, are consolidated and published by Sringeri Math. This compilation is named 'Sri Dakṣiṇāmūrti Stotram', with the translation credited to Dr. D.S. Subbramaiya. He is known for his contributions to the study of Advaita Vedanta. His work on the Sri Dakṣiṇāmūrti Stotram stands out as a noteworthy contribution to understanding this intricate hymn. While Adi Shankaracharya's Dakṣiṇāmūrti Stotram and its associated commentaries remain primary sources for Advaita Vedanta's teachings, Dr. Subbaramaiya's exposition offers a bridge between traditional perspectives and modern philosophical thought.

4. Sri Dakṣiṇāmūrti Stotram Bhashya by Swami Harshananda: This commentary, in line with the tradition of Shankara's bhashyas (commentaries), offers explanations for the verses, helping the reader understand the philosophical underpinnings of the Stotram. Swami Harshananda was the 10th President of the Ramakrishna Math and Ramakrishna Mission and was distinguished for

his profound expertise in Vedanta philosophy and deep spiritual commitment.

5. Dakṣiṇāmūrti Stotram with Gaudapadacharya's Karika by Swami Chinmāyananda: In this work, Swami Chinmāyananda provides a modern interpretation of the Stotram, combining the traditional teachings with explanations relevant for the contemporary audience.

6. Commentaries by Other Scholars: Apart from Sureshvara, other scholars have also written vārtikas on the Dakṣiṇāmūrti Stotram. These vārtikas, by their very nature, not only offer explanations but also elaborate on the Stotram's teachings, filling in perceived gaps or clarifying subtle points.

Several regional scholars and spiritual leaders might have penned down their reflections, commentaries, or translations on the Dakṣiṇāmūrti Stotram. Many of these writings might be in regional languages or might not have gained international prominence. For an exhaustive list, institutions that focus on Vedanta, libraries with a strong Indology section, or publishers that specialize in Vedanta scriptures might provide a more comprehensive collection.

Given the Stotram's depth and its position as a seminal text in Advaita Vedanta, these commentaries play a pivotal role in ensuring its teachings are accessible, understandable, and relevant across generations. They allow scholars, students, and spiritual seekers to engage deeply with the Stotram, offering varied perspectives on its profound truths.

Chapter 5

TRANSLITERATION, TRANSLATION AND MEANING

‖ शान्तिपाठः ‖

śāntipāṭhaḥ

ॐ यो ब्रह्माणं विदधाति पूर्वम्
यो वै वेदांश्च प्रहिणोति तस्मै ।
तं ह देवमात्मबुद्धिप्रकाशं
मुमुक्षुर्वै शरणमहं प्रपद्ये ‖
ॐ शान्तिः शान्तिः शान्तिः

Om yo brahmāṇaṁ vidadhāti pūrvam
yo vai vedāṁśca prahiṇoti tasmai I
taṁ ha devamātmabuddhiprakāśaṁ
mumukṣurvai śaraṇamahaṁ prapadye II
Om śāntiḥ śāntiḥ śāntiḥ

Meaning

ॐ (Om) - The universal sound symbolizing the ultimate reality; यो=यः (yo=yaḥ) – Who; ब्रह्माणं (brahmāṇam) – Brahma (one of the Trimurti, the creator godhead); विदधाति (vidadhāti) - ordained; पूर्वम् (pūrvam) - In the beginning; यो=यः (yo=yaḥ) – Who; वै (vai) – Indeed; वेदांश्च (vedāṃśca) - The Vedas also; प्रहिणोति (prahiṇoti) – Teaches; तस्मै (tasmai) - To Him; तं (taṃ) – Him; ह (ha) – Verily (indeed); देवम् (devam) - The Divine; आत्म-बुद्धि-प्रकाशं (ātma-buddhi-prakāśaṃ) - The enlightener of inner wisdom; मुमुक्षुर्वै (mumukṣurvai) - Desiring liberation indeed; शरणमहं (śaraṇamahaṃ) - I take refuge; प्रपद्ये (prapadye) - I resort to; ॐ शान्तिः शान्तिः शान्तिः (Om śāntiḥ śāntiḥ śāntiḥ) - Om Peace Peace Peace

Who before creation, ordains the cosmic order (Brahma)
Who indeed propagates the knowledge of the Vedas,
To that divine entity who illuminates (one's) intellect
I, the one desiring liberation, take refuge and surrender.
Om, Peace, Peace, Peace.

Commentary

This verse praises the divine entity responsible for the creation and order of the universe and the propagation of spiritual knowledge. The seeker acknowledges the divine illumination of self-consciousness and expresses a desire for liberation, surrendering to the divine presence. The repetition of "Peace" at the end seeks harmony and tranquility in mind, body, and spirit.

Buddhi, here, denotes the intellectual faculty and the ability to reason, discern, or judge.

This śāntipāṭhaḥ invokes peace and expresses a longing for ultimate knowledge and liberation. It refers to the divine principle that governs the universe and reveals the wisdom of the Vedas. The chant ends with a call for peace, symbolizing harmony with the cosmic order. It expresses the seeker's humble surrender to the ultimate reality, seeking the illumination of wisdom and the desire for liberation.

ध्यानश्लोकाः

Dhyānaślokāḥ

मौनव्याख्याप्रकटितपरब्रह्मतत्त्वं युवानं
वर्षिष्ठान्ते वसदृषिगणैरावृतं ब्रह्मनिष्ठैः ।
आचार्येन्द्रं करकलितचिन्मुद्रमानन्दरूपं
स्वात्मारामं मुदितवदनं दक्षिणामूर्तिमीडे ॥१॥

Mounavyākhyāprakaṭitaparabrahmatattvaṃ yuvānaṃ

Varṣiṣṭhānte vasadṛṣigaṇairāvṛtaṃ brahmaniṣṭhaiḥ

Ācāryendraṃ karakalitachinmudramānandarūpaṃ

Swātmārāmaṃ muditavādanaṃ dakṣiṇāmūrtimīḍe II 1 II

Word-by-word breakdown

मौन-व्याख्या प्रकटित परब्रह्म-तत्त्वं युवानं

वर्षिष्ठ-अंते वसत् ऋषि-गणैः आवृतं ब्रह्म-निष्ठैः ।

आचार्य-इंद्रं कर-कलित-चिन्मुद्रं-आनन्द-रूपं

स्व-आत्मा-रामं मुदित-वदनं दक्षिणा-मूर्तिं ईडे ॥१॥

mauna-vyākhyā prakaṭita parabrahma-tattvaṁ yuvānaṁ

varṣiṣṭha-ante vasat ṛṣi-gaṇaiḥ āvṛtaṁ brahma-niṣṭhaiḥ

ācārya-indraṁ kara-kalita-cinmudraṁ-ānanda-rūpaṁ

sva-ātmā-rāmaṁ mudita-vādanaṁ dakṣiṇā-mūrtiṁ īḍe II 1 II

Meaning

मौन-व्याख्या (mauna-vyākhyā): explanation through silence; प्रकटित (prakaṭita): Revealed; परब्रह्म-तत्त्वं (parabrahma tattvam): Supreme Brahman principle; युवानं (yuvānaṃ): Young; वर्षिष्ठ-अन्ते (varṣiṣṭha-ante) - at the end of the age (typically referring to a very old age or time); वसत् (vasat): dwelling, residing; ऋषि-गणैः (ṛṣi-gaṇaiḥ): by groups of seers or sages; आवृतं (āvṛtaṃ): surrounded or enveloped; ब्रह्म-निष्ठैः (brahma-niṣṭhaiḥ): by those who are firmly established in Brahman; आचार्य-इन्द्रं (ācārya-indraṃ): The chief of teachers; कर-कलित-चिन्मुद्रं-आनन्द-रूपं (kara-kalita-cinmudram-ānandarūpam): Forming the gesture of knowledge, blissful form; स्वात्मा-रामं (svātmā-rāmam): Reveling in one's own self; मुदित-वदनं (muditavādanaṃ): with a joyful or pleased face (or facial expression); दक्षिणा-मूर्तिम् (dakṣiṇā-mūrtim): Dakṣiṇāmūrti; ईडे (īḍe): I praise

The youth who explains the supreme truth of Brahman through silence

Surrounded by aged sages and steadfast in Brahman,

The king of teachers, whose hand holds the pose of knowledge, and whose form is pure bliss

Self-contented, with a cheerful face, I praise Dakṣiṇāmūrti.

Commentary

The verse is a praise of Sri Dakṣiṇāmūrti, the form of Shiva as the supreme teacher. It describes Dakṣiṇāmūrti as young sage (guru) surrounded by wise sages and steadfast in the truth of Brahman. He reveals the supreme principle through silence and is depicted with a gesture of knowledge, embodying joy, and reveling in His own self.

मौन-व्याख्या प्रकटित परब्रह्म-तत्त्वं युवानं

mauna-vyākhyā prakaṭita parabrahma-tattvaṁ yuvānaṁ

The sage's wisdom is conveyed not through speech, but through the state of silence. This suggests that the sage has realized the ultimate truth beyond the limitations of language. The term "parabrahma-tattvam" refers to the absolute reality beyond the manifested world. The sage is described as youthful, indicating that despite age, His inner state is ever fresh and vibrant due to His profound understanding.

वर्षिष्ठ-अंते वसत् ऋषि-गणैः आवृतं ब्रह्म-निष्ठैः

varṣiṣṭha-aṁte vasat ṛṣi-gaṇaiḥ āvṛtaṁ brahma-niṣṭhaiḥ

In their old age, the sage is surrounded by a gathering of wise sages who are also deeply devoted to the understanding of Brahman. This portrays the sage as a respected teacher who attracts fellow seekers due to their profound spiritual insights.

आचार्य-इंद्रं कर-कलित-चिन्मुद्रं-आनन्द-रूपं

ācārya-indraṁ kara-kalita-cinmudraṁ ānanda-rūpaṁ

The sage is depicted as the foremost among teachers, adorned with a "chinmudra" (gesture symbolizing unity-consciousness). This signifies His mastery over the knowledge of consciousness. The sage's form is described as an embodiment of joy and bliss.

स्व-आत्मा-रामं मुदित-वदनं दक्षिणा-मूर्तिं ईडे

sva-ātmā-rāmaṁ mudita-vādanaṁ dakṣiṇā-mūrtiṁ īḍe

The sage rejoices in their own self (Ātman), reflecting His self-contentment. His countenance is filled with joy. The reference to Dakṣiṇāmūrti alludes to the image of the divine teacher imparting wisdom in silence. The poet expresses reverence and salutation to this sage.

The verse is dedicated to Sri Dakṣiṇāmūrti, a form of Shiva that represents the supreme teacher. It emphasizes the profound silence through which the ultimate truth of Brahman is conveyed, reflecting a core concept in Advaita Vedanta where silence is considered the most eloquent expression of the indescribable absolute.

The word "ईडे" (īḍe), at the end of each sloka, is derived from the root verb "ईड्" (īḍ), which means "to praise" or "to eulogize". The form "ईडे" is a first-person singular form, which translates to "I praise" or "I adore".

The phrase करकलितचिन्मुद्रमानन्दरूपं (kara-kalita-cinmudraṁ-ānanda-rūpaṁ) essentially describes a form that is exuding bliss and has a hand positioned in the Chinmudra gesture. In many contexts, especially related to the representation of deities like Dakṣiṇāmūrti, this refers to the divine form of the deity exhibiting supreme bliss and holding the Chinmudra gesture with the hand.

The imagery in this verse shows Dakṣiṇāmūrti as youthful and surrounded by wise sages like Vashistha. He's depicted holding the Chinmudra, a hand gesture that symbolizes the oneness of the individual soul and the supreme soul. His joyful face and self-contentment signify his perfect understanding and embodiment of the ultimate reality.

Overall, the verse is a beautiful homage to Dakṣiṇāmūrti's role as a divine guide in the spiritual journey, leading seekers to the profound realization of non-duality.

वटविटपिसमीपे भूमिभागे निषण्णं
सकलमुनिजनानां ज्ञानदातारमारात् ।
त्रिभुवनगुरुमीशं दक्षिणामूर्तिदेवं
जननमरणदुःखच्छेददक्षं नमामि ॥ २ ॥

vaṭaviṭapisamīpe bhūmibhāge niṣaṇṇaṃ

sakalamunijanānāṃ jñānadātāramārāt

tribhuvanagurumīśaṃ dakṣiṇāmūrtidevaṃ

jananamaraṇaduḥkhacchedadakṣaṃ namāmi II 2 II

Word-by-word breakdown

वट-विटपि-समीपे भूमि-भागे निषण्णं
सकल-मुनि-जनानां ज्ञान-दातारम्-आरात् ।
त्रि-भुवन-गुरुम् ईशं दक्षिणा-मूर्ति-देवं
जनन-मरण-दुःख-छेद-दक्षं नमामि ॥ २ ॥

vaṭa-viṭapi-samīpe bhūmi-bhāge niṣaṇṇaṃ

sakala-muni-janānaṃ jñāna-dātāram-ārāt

tri-bhuvana-gurum īśaṃ dakṣiṇā-mūrti-devaṃ

janana-maraṇa-duḥkha-cheda-dakṣaṃ namāmi II 2 II

Meaning

वट-विटपि-समीपे (vaṭa-viṭapi-samīpe): Near the banyan tree; भूमि-भागे (bhūmi-bhāge): On the ground; निषण्णं (niṣaṇṇaṃ): Seated; सकल-मुनि-जनानां (sakala-muni-janānāṃ): For all sages; ज्ञान-दातारम्-आरात् (jñāna-dātāram-ārāt): Bestower of wisdom; त्रि-भुवन-गुरुम्-ईशं (tri-bhuvana-gurum-īśaṃ): The Guru of the three worlds; दक्षिणा-मूर्ति-देवं (dakṣiṇā-mūrti-devaṃ): The deity Dakṣiṇāmūrti; जनन-मरण-दुःख-च्छेद-दक्षं (janana-maraṇa-duḥkha-ccheda-dakṣaṃ): The adept in removing the sorrow of birth and death; नमामि (namāmi): I salute

Seated at the base of the banyan tree.

The bestower of knowledge to all sages.

The teacher of the three worlds, Sri Dakṣiṇāmūrti .

I bow to Him who is skilled in dispelling the sorrows of birth and death

Commentary

The verse is a salutation to Sri Dakṣiṇāmūrti, a form of Lord Shiva as the universal teacher. It portrays him as seated near a banyan tree, symbolizing wisdom. The banyan tree, with its extensive root system, is often taken as a symbol for eternal life and spiritual growth. The verse recognizes Dakṣiṇāmūrti as the giver of knowledge to all sages, the master of the three worlds, and the one who has the power to alleviate the sufferings of life and death. The imagery of the banyan tree and the grounding to the earth underscores a connection to nature and the physical embodiment of spiritual truths.

वट-विटपि-समीपे भूमि-भागे निषण्णं

vata-viṭapi-samīpe bhūmi-bhāge niṣaṇṇaṃ

The verse opens with a description of the location, indicating that the sage is seated under the sacred banyan tree (vata) in a particular place on the ground.

सकल-मुनि-जनानां ज्ञान-दातारम्-आरात्

sakala-muni-janānāṁ jñāna-dātāram-ārāt

The sage is hailed as the bestower of knowledge for all sages and people. The term "ārāt" signifies the poet's reverence and approach to this sage for gaining wisdom.

त्रि-भुवन-गुरुम् ईशं दक्षिणा-मूर्ति-देवं

tri-bhuvana-gurum īśaṁ dakṣiṇā-mūrti-devaṁ

The sage is revered as the guru (teacher) of the three worlds, embodying the divine essence of Lord Shiva in the form of Dakṣiṇāmūrti, the supreme teacher.

जनन-मरण-दुःख-छेद-दक्षं नमामि

janan-marana-duḥkha-chheda-dakṣaṁ namāmi

The sage is honored as one who possesses the skill to alleviate the pains of birth and death, signifying their role as a spiritual guide who helps transcend the cycle of life and death.

This verse venerates the sage seated under the banyan tree as the giver of knowledge, the Guru of the three worlds, and a compassionate guide who leads seekers out of the cycle of suffering and ignorance. The poet approaches this sage with deep reverence for their spiritual wisdom and guidance.

चित्रं वटतरोर्मूले वृद्धाः शिष्या गुरुर्युवा ।

गुरोऽस्तु मौनं व्याख्यानं शिष्यास्तु छिन्न संशयाः ॥ ३॥

chitraṃ vaṭatarormūle vṛddhāḥ śiṣyā gururyuvā

guro'stu maunaṃ vyākhyānaṃ śiṣyāstu chinna saṃśayāḥ II 3 II

Word-by-word breakdown

चित्रं वट-तरोः-मूले वृद्धाः शिष्याः गुरुः युवा ।

गुरोः अस्तु मौनं व्याख्यानं शिष्याः तु छिन्न-संशयाः ॥ ३॥

chitraṃ vaṭa-taroh-mūle vṛddhāḥ śiṣyāḥ guruḥ yuvā I

guroh astu maunaṃ vyākhyānaṃ śiṣyāḥ tu chinna-saṃśayāḥ II 3 II

Meaning

चित्रं (citram): Picture, scenario; वट-तरोः-मूले (vaṭa-taroh-mūle): Under the Banyan tree; वृद्धाः (vṛddhāḥ): Old; शिष्या (śiṣyā): Disciples; गुरुः-युवा (guruḥ-yuvā): Guru (is) young; गुरोः अस्तु (guroh astu): Guru indeed; मौनं (maunaṃ): Silence; व्याख्यानं (vyākhyānaṃ): Explanation; शिष्याः तु (śiṣyāḥ tu): Disciples indeed; छिन्न संशयाः (chinna saṃśayāḥ): (are) devoid of doubts.

Below the banyan tree, a picture (imagery) emerges,

Where disciples are elderly, and the guru is youthful.

The guru's teachings are conveyed in silence,

And the disciples are left without any doubts.

Commentary

This verse paints a vivid picture of the teaching of Sri Dakṣiṇāmūrti , the universal Guru. Seated under a banyan tree, the youthful Guru imparts wisdom to his aged disciples through the profound language of silence. Throug

h this silent communion, the doubts and uncertainties of the disciples are cleared away.

चित्रं वट-तरोः-मूले वृद्धाः शिष्याः गुरुः युवा

chitram vaṭa-taroḥ-mūle vṛddhāḥ śiṣyāḥ guruḥ yuvā

The scene is set under a colorful banyan tree, where a group of aged disciples and a young Guru have gathered.

गुरोः अस्तु मौनं व्याख्यानं शिष्याः तु छिन्न-संशयाः

guroḥ astu maunaṁ vyākhyānaṁ śiṣyāḥ tu chhinna-saṁśayāḥ

The Guru is to maintain silence, indicating that their wisdom is beyond verbal expression. The disciples, on the other hand, have their doubts removed, symbolizing their readiness to receive knowledge.

This shloka depicts an educational scene under a banyan tree where a young Guru sits with elderly disciples. The Guru's silence implies that their wisdom transcends words, while the disciples, their doubts cleared, are prepared to absorb knowledge. It underscores the profound connection between the Guru and the disciples in the quest for learning and understanding.

The symbolism here runs deep, reflecting themes of eternal wisdom, transcending age, and the power of silent understanding. It's often seen as a metaphor for how profound truths are grasped beyond words, through direct experience and realization.

निधये सर्वविद्यानां भिषजे भवरोगिणाम् ।
गुरवे सर्वलोकानां दक्षिणामूर्तये नमः ॥ ४॥
Nidhaye sarvavidyānāṁ bhiṣaje bhavarogiṇām |
Gurave sarvalokānāṁ dakṣiṇāmūrtaye namaḥ II 4 II

Word-by-word breakdown

निधये सर्व-विद्यानां भिषजे भव-रोगिणाम्।
गुरवे सर्व-लोकानां दक्षिणामूर्तये-नमः ॥ ४॥
Nidhaye Sarva-vidyānāṁ Bhiṣaje Bhava-rogiṇām|
Gurave Sarva-lokānāṁ Dakṣiṇāmūrtaye Namaḥ ॥

Meaning

निधये (nidhaye): Treasure; सर्व-विद्यानां (sarva-vidyānāṁ): Of all knowledge; भिषजे (bhiṣaje): Doctor; भव-रोगिणाम् (bhava-roṅiṇām): Of the disease of worldly existence; गुरवे (gurave): To the Guru; सर्व-लोकानां (sarva-lokānaṁ): Of all the worlds; दक्षिणामूर्तये (dakṣiṇāmūrtaye): To Dakṣiṇāmūrti; नमः (namaḥ): Salutation.

The treasure trove of all knowledge

The healer for the disease of worldly existence

The Guru (teacher) of all the worlds

Salutations to Dakṣiṇāmūrti

Commentary

In essence, the verse is an expression of reverence to Sri Dakṣiṇāmūrti. He is depicted as the embodiment of wisdom, the divine healer of existential ailments, and the supreme teacher for all beings in the universe. By addressing Dakṣiṇāmūrti with these epithets, the verse conveys the universal and eternal role of the deity as a guide, healer, and enlightener. It reflects a profound spiritual concept in which knowledge is seen as both a path to transcendence and a remedy for worldly suffering.

निधये सर्व-विद्यानां भिषजे भव-रोगिणाम्।
nidhaye sarva-vidyānāṁ bhiṣaje bhava-rogiṇām

This line is a salutation to the divine Guru who is the source of all knowledge and the healer of those suffering from the cycle of birth and death (Samsāra).

गुरवे सर्व-लोकानां दक्षिणामूर्तये-नमः॥
gurave sarva-lokānāṁ dakṣiṇāmūrtaye-namaḥ

The second line pays homage to the Guru who is the teacher for all beings across all worlds, manifesting as Dakṣiṇāmūrti, who is a form of Lord Shiva imparting wisdom in silence.

This shloka expresses deep reverence to the Guru as the repository of all knowledge, the healer of worldly suffering, and the universal teacher guiding all beings. It highlights the Guru's role in imparting wisdom and guiding individuals toward liberation from the cycle of birth and death.

ॐ नमः प्रणवार्थाय शुद्धज्ञानैकमूर्तये ।
निर्मलाय प्रशान्ताय दक्षिणामूर्तये नमः ॥ ५॥

Om namaḥ praṇavārthāya śuddhajñānaikamūrtaye |
Nirmalāya praśāntāya dakṣiṇāmūrtaye namaḥ II 5 II

Word-by-word breakdown

ॐ नमः प्रणव-अर्थाय शुद्ध-ज्ञान-एक-मूर्तये ।
निर्मलाय प्रशान्ताय दक्षिणा-मूर्तये-नमः ॥ ५॥

Om Namah Praṇava-arthāya Shuddha-jñāna-eka-mūrtaye |
Nirmalāya Praśāntāya Dakṣiṇā-mūrtaye-Namah || 5 ||

Meaning

ॐ (oṃ): Sacred sound; नमः (namaḥ): Salutation; प्रणव-अर्थाय (praṇava-arthāya): To the meaning of Om; शुद्ध-ज्ञान-एक-

मूर्तये (śuddha-jñāna-eka-mūrtaye): To the one form of pure knowledge; निर्मलाय (nirmalāya): To the unblemished one; प्रशान्ताय (praśāntāya): To the peaceful one; दक्षिणामूर्तये (dakṣiṇāmūrtaye): To Dakṣiṇāmūrti; नमः (namaḥ): Salutation

Salutations to the one who represents the pure knowledge and essence of the sacred syllable Om, embodying its singular form.

To the one who is pure, calm, and serene; Salutations to Dakṣiṇāmūrti.

Commentary

This verse is offering salutations to Sri Dakṣiṇāmūrti, depicting him as the embodiment of the profound meaning behind the sacred syllable 'Om.' He represents the essence of pure knowledge, free from all impurities, and embodies serenity and tranquility. Again, the focus is on the supreme wisdom and spirituality that Sri Dakṣiṇāmūrti symbolizes. The verse serves to invoke his presence and blessings, recognizing his unparalleled role as a divine teacher and guide.

ॐ नमः प्रणव-अर्थाय शुद्ध-ज्ञान-एक-मूर्तये।

om namaḥ praṇava-arthāya śuddha-jñāna-eka-mūrtaye

This line pays homage to the embodiment of pure knowledge, represented by the sacred syllable 'Om'. The Guru is seen as the embodiment of the profound wisdom represented by the primordial sound 'Om'.

निर्मलाय प्रशान्ताय दक्षिणा-मूर्तये - नमः॥

nirmalāya prashāntāya dakṣiṇā-mūrtaye - namaḥ

The second line reveres the Guru as the embodiment of purity and serenity, likened to the form of Dakṣiṇāmūrti.

This shloka acknowledges the Guru's embodiment of pure knowledge and serene wisdom. It recognizes the Guru as the representation of the profound sound 'Om' and draws a parallel between the Guru and the divine form of Dakṣiṇāmūrti. The shloka captures the essence of the Guru's wisdom and his transformative presence.

The last three verses are dedicated to Sri Dakṣiṇāmūrti, a form of Lord Shiva. They describe the scene where the young Guru (Sri Dakṣiṇāmūrti) imparts wisdom to the old disciples through silence, and they praise Him as the treasure of all knowledge, the healer of worldly ailments, the embodiment of pure knowledge, and the unblemished and peaceful one.

दक्षिणामूर्तिस्तोत्रं

Dakṣiṇāmūrti Stotram

विश्वं दर्पणदृश्यमाननगरीतुल्यं निजान्तर्गतं
पश्यन्नात्मनि मायया बहिरिवोद्भूतं यथा निद्रया।
यः साक्षात्कुरुते प्रबोधसमये स्वात्मानमेवाद्वयं
तस्मै श्रीगुरुमूर्तये नम इदं श्रीदक्षिणामूर्तये ॥ १ ॥

visvaṁ darpaṇadṛśyamānanagarītulyaṁ nijāntargataṁ
paśyannātmani māyayā bahirivodbhūtaṁ yathā nidrayā I
yaḥ sākṣātkurute prabodhasamaye svātmānamevādvayaṁ
tasmai śrīgurumūrtaye nama idaṁ śrīdakṣiṇāmūrtaye II 1 II

Word-by-word breakdown

विश्वं दर्पण-दृश्यमान-नगरी-तुल्यं निज-अन्तर्गतं
पश्यन् आत्मनि मायया बहिः इव उद्भूतं यथा निद्रया।
यः साक्षात्-कुरुते प्रबोध-समये स्व-आत्मानम् एव अद्वयं
तस्मै श्री-गुरु-मूर्तये नमः इदं श्री-दक्षिणा-मूर्तये॥ १॥

visvaṁ darpaṇa-dṛśya-māna-nagarī-tulyaṁ nija-antargataṁ
paśyan ātmani māyayā bahiḥ iva udbhūtaṁ yathā nidrayā I
yaḥ sākṣāt-kurute prabodha-samaye sva-ātmānam eva
advayaṁ
tasmai śrī-guru-mūrtaye namaḥ idaṁ śrī-dakṣiṇā-mūrtaye II 1 II

Meaning

विश्वं (Viśvaṁ): Universe; दर्पण (Darpaṇa): Mirror; दृश्यमान (Dṛśyamāna): Seen; नगरी (Nagarī): City; तुल्यं (Tulyaṁ): Similar; निज-अंतर्गतं (nija-antargataṁ): Inside oneself; पश्यन् (Paśyann): Seeing; आत्मनि (Ātmani): In oneself; मायया (Māyayā): With illusion; बहिः-इव (bahiḥ-iva): As if outside; उद्भूतं (Udbhūtaṁ): Manifested; यथा (Yathā): Like; निद्रया (Nidrayā): In sleep; यः (Yaḥ): Who; साक्षात् कुरुते (sākṣāt kurute): Realizes directly; प्रबोधसमये (Prabodhasamaye): At the time of awakening; स्व-आत्मानम् (Swa-ātmānam): The self; एव (Eva): Only; अद्वयं (Advayam): Non-dual; तस्मै

(Tasmai): To that; श्रीगुरुमूर्तये (Śrīgurumūrtaye): To the form of the honorable Guru; नमः (Namaḥ): Salutation; इदं (Idam): This; श्रीदक्षिणामूर्तये (Śrīdakṣiṇāmūrtaye): To Shri Dakṣiṇāmūrti

> *The universe is like a city seen in a mirror, situated within oneself.*
>
> *Perceiving with the illusion (Māya) in oneself as though it has emerged outside, just as in a dream.*
>
> *Who, during the time of awakening, realizes the non-dual nature of the Self.*
>
> *To that auspicious Guru form, I offer my salutations, to the revered Dakṣiṇāmūrti .*

To the esteemed Sri Dakhinamurthi, the revered Guru, who, during moments of spiritual awakening, perceives the non-dual essence of the Self. He understands the world as existing within oneself, mirroring a city's reflection, yet seemingly projected outward through the illusion of "maya", much like a dream.

Commentary

The verse draws an analogy between the world and a reflection in a mirror, portraying the world as a manifestation within oneself. It alludes to the concept of Māya or illusion, where the external world is perceived as a dreamlike state. Sri Dakṣiṇāmūrti, as the ultimate Guru, imparts the realization of the non-dual nature of the Self, helping the seeker awaken from this illusion. The verse is a profound homage to Dakṣiṇāmūrti's wisdom and guidance, recognizing his role in leading one toward the true understanding of reality.

विश्वं दर्पणदृश्यमाननगरीतुल्यं निजान्तर्गतं
viśvaṁ darpaṇadṛśyamānanagarītulyaṁ nijāntargataṁ

The universe (viśvaṁ) is likened to a city (nagarī) seen in a mirror (darpaṇa). This analogy suggests that the vast external universe is reflective of the internal self. Just as the reflection in the mirror is not different from the mirror, the manifested universe is not separate from the Self; it is contained within our very being (nijāntargataṁ).

पश्यन्नात्मनि मायया बहिरिवोद्भूतं यथा निद्रया
paśyannātmani māyayā bahirivodbhūtaṁ yathā nidrayā

The universe, though appearing external (bahiriva), is perceived internally (ātmani) due to the play of māyā (illusion). This can be likened to the phenomenon of dreams (nidrayā) where entire worlds manifest and are experienced within, even though they appear to be outside of oneself.

पश्यन्नात्मनि मायया बहिरिवोद्भूतं (paśyannātmani māyayā bahirivodbhūtaṁ) speaks to how, under the sway of māyā, the internal essence (Brahman) seems to manifest externally as the world. It's a mirroring of the inside to the outside, but this external reality is not truly separate or different from the inner self; it only appears so. यथा निद्रया

(yathā nidrayā) draws a parallel between our everyday experiences in the world and dream states. Just as dreams appear real and tangible when we're within them but are recognized as illusory upon waking, the world, under the influence of māyā, appears real. However, in moments of deep insight or realization, one might recognize its ephemeral and illusory nature, just like a dream upon waking.

In the philosophy of Advaita Vedanta, the ultimate goal is self-realization or the realization of the non-dual nature of existence, where one perceives no distinction between the individual self (ātman) and the universal consciousness (Brahman). This verse highlights the challenge on this path: the pervasive and deceptive influence of māyā that makes the non-dual appear dual, the internal appear external, and the unreal appear real.

In essence, this part of the verse serves as a contemplative reminder of the complexities and challenges of spiritual realization within the framework of Advaita Vedanta. It underscores the need for discernment and the deep introspection required to see beyond the illusory play of māyā and recognize the true, undivided nature of reality.

यः साक्षात्कुरुते प्रबोधसमये स्वात्मानमेवाद्वयं

yaḥ sākṣātkurute prabodhasamaye svātmānamevādvayaṁ

At the time of true awakening (prabodhasamaye), one realizes directly (sākṣāt kurute) that the Self (svātmānam) is the only non-dual (advayam) reality. This awakening transcends the dualistic perceptions and reveals the inherent oneness of all existence.

This verse speaks to that profound moment of realization or enlightenment (prabodhasamaye, प्रबोधसमये). At this moment, the seeker or the individual (who, यः) directly perceives or realizes (sākṣāt kurute, साक्षात्कुरुते) their true nature. They see that their innermost self is not different from the ultimate reality. They understand that their Ātman is Brahman, undifferentiated and non-dual (advayam, अद्वयं).

This realization contrasts with the ordinary state of human consciousness, where individuals often perceive themselves as separate from the world around them and the divine. Such duality is seen as a result of ignorance (avidyā) in Advaita Vedanta.

In essence, the verse encapsulates the pinnacle of spiritual realization: the direct perception of one's true, non-dual nature during moments of profound awakening. It signifies the shedding of illusory beliefs and the embracing of an undivided reality, where the distinction between the self and the universe dissolves.

तस्मै श्रीगुरुमूर्तये नम इदं श्रीदक्षिणामूर्तये
tasmai śrīgurumūrtaye nama idaṁ śrīdakṣiṇāmūrtaye

The verse concludes with a salutation and homage to the Guru, embodied as Dakṣiṇāmūrti, the personification of divine knowledge and wisdom. It is through the grace and teachings of this Guru that seekers are led to the profound realization of non-duality and the true nature of the Self.

In summary, this verse elucidates the idea that the vast universe, though appearing external, is a reflection of the inner Self, shaped by the play of māyā. Through true awakening, facilitated by the grace of the Guru, one realizes the non-dual nature of existence, transcending the illusory dichotomies of inside and outside. Top of Form

Overall, this sloka beautifully captures the essence of Advaita Vedanta, emphasizing the intrinsic non-dual nature of the Self, the play of Māya, and the pivotal role of the Guru in aiding spiritual awakening.

बीजस्यान्तरिवाङ्कुरो जगदिदं प्राङ्निर्विकल्पं पुनः
मायाकल्पितदेशकालकलनावैचित्र्यचित्रीकृतम् ।
मायावीव विजृम्भयत्यपि महायोगीव यः स्वेच्छया
तस्मै श्रीगुरुमूर्तये नम इदं श्रीदक्षिणामूर्तये ॥ २ ॥

bījasyāntarivaṅkuro jagadidaṃ prāṅnirvikalpaṃ punaḥ

māyākalpitadeśakālakalanāvaicitryacitrīkṛtam

māyāvīva vijṛmbhayatyapi mahāyogīva yaḥ svechchayā

tasmai śrīgurumūrtaye nama idaṃ śrīdakṣiṇāmūrtaye II 2 II

Word-by-word breakdown

बीजस्य अंतः इव अंकुरः जगद् इदं प्राक् निर्विकल्पं पुनः
माया-कल्पित-देश-काल-कलना-वैचित्र्य-चित्रीकृतम् ।
मायावी इव विजृम्भयति अपि महा-योगी इव यः स्व-इच्छया
तस्मै श्री-गुरु-मूर्तये नमः इदं श्री-दक्षिणा-मूर्तये ॥ २ ॥

bījasya antaḥ iva aṅkuraḥ jagad idaṁ prāk nirvikalpaṁ punaḥ

māyā-kalpita-deśa-kāla-kalanā-vaicitrya-citrīkṛtam

māyāvī iva vijṛmbhayati api mahā-yogī iva yaḥ sva-icchayā

tasmai śrī-guru-mūrtaye namaḥ idaṁ śrī-dakṣiṇā-mūrtaye

II 2 II

Meaning

बीजस्य (Bījasya): Of the seed; अंतः इव (Antara iva): Inside like; अंकुरः (aṅkuraha): Sprout; जगदिदं (Jagadidam): This world; प्राक् (Prāk): Before; निर्विकल्पं (Nirvikalpam): Without differentiation; पुनः (Punaḥ): Again; मायाकल्पित (Māyākalpita): Imagined by Māya (illusion); देशकालकलना (Deśakālakalanā): Calculations of space and time; वैचित्र्य (Vaicitrya): Diversity; चित्रीकृतम् (Citrikṛtam): Painted; मायावी इव (Māyāvī iva): Magician like; विजृम्भयति अपि (vijṛmbhayati api): Expands; महायोगी (Mahāyogī): Great Yogi; इव (iva): like; यः (yah) = who; स्व-इच्छया (sva-icchayā): With one's own will; तस्मै (Tasmai): To that; श्रीगुरुमूर्तये (Śrīgurumūrtaye): To the divine form of the Guru; नमः (Namaḥ): Salutation; इदं (Idam): This; श्रीदक्षिणामूर्तये (Śrīdakṣiṇāmūrtaye): To Sri Dakṣiṇāmūrti.

Like the sprout inside a seed. This world, before appearing as it does, was undifferentiated.

Crafted with the distinctions of space and time, and variegated by the diverse play of Māya.

It manifests as if by magic. Or by the will of a great yogi.

To that revered form of the Guru, I bow. This is to the esteemed Dakṣiṇāmūrti.

Commentary

To the venerable Sri Dakhinamurthi, the exalted Guru, who, by his own free will, conjures this world like a magician or yogi. Before its creation, it existed seamlessly, akin to a sprout inside a seed, but with its interplay with space and time, facilitated by Māya, it evolved into varied forms.

बीजस्यान्तरिवाङ्कुरो जगदिदं प्राङ्निर्विकल्पं पुनः

bījasyāntarivaṅkuro jagadidaṁ prāṅnirvikalpaṁ punaḥ

The phrase can be roughly translated as: "Just as a sprout is contained within a seed, so too is this undifferentiated world contained within its source before manifesting again."

The world (jagadidaṁ) is likened to a sprout (aṅkura) emerging from within a seed (bījasya). This implies the latent potential and essence of the universe existing inherently within its primordial state. Just as the sprout manifests from the potential contained in the seed, the universe emerges from a primal, undifferentiated state (nirvikalpa).

The metaphor of a seed and its sprout is used to elucidate the nature of the universe and its source. Just as the potentiality of the sprout (the universe in its manifested form) is contained within the seed (the source or the primordial state) in an undifferentiated form, so too is the universe contained within its original source before it manifests.

The phrase also implies the cyclical nature of creation, sustenance, and dissolution in Hindu cosmology. Before the universe comes into existence in its differentiated and manifold form, it exists in a potential, unmanifested, and undifferentiated state within its source. This source or primordial essence can be likened to Brahman in Advaita Vedanta or the supreme reality in various other traditions.

In essence, the universe's manifestation is not seen as creation ex nihilo (out of nothing) but as an unfolding or manifestation of what already existed in potential. Just as the tree exists in potential within the seed, the universe existed in potential within Brahman, the ultimate reality.

The Chāndogya Upanishad, one of the major Upanishads, delves deep into the nature of existence and the origin of the universe. The Upanishad postulates that the entire universe existed in potential within the singular reality of Sat or Existence.

In the Upanishad, there's the famous declaration: सदेव सोम्येदमग्र आसीदेकमेवाद्वितीयम् sadeva somyedamagra āsīdekamevādvitīyam (6.2.1-3). This translates to: "O good-looking one, before this (world began), there was only Existence (Sat), one without a second."

The Chāndogya Upanishad employs various analogies to explain the transformation of the one undifferentiated reality into the manifold universe. For instance, it uses the example of clay and clay objects, gold and gold ornaments, and iron and iron tools to illustrate that the essence remains unchanged even though forms may vary. Just as the potential form of an ornament exists within gold, the potential for the universe existed within Sat. This understanding aligns with the core teachings of Advaita Vedanta, which posits that the ultimate reality (Brahman) is non-dual, and everything we perceive is a manifestation of that singular reality.

The word निर्विकल्पं (Nirvikalpam) in this verse deserves a special mention. It means, no विकल्प (vikalpa) or no change or distinction. It refers to that which is beyond any conceptual distinction or duality. One of the states of consciousness that a practitioner or meditator (in yogic practices) can experience is निर्विकल्प समाधि (Nirvikalpa Samādhi). In this state, the individual loses awareness of all dualities and distinctions, experiencing a profound union with the universal consciousness or Brahman. There's no sense of individual self ('I', 'me', 'mine') or any perception of the external world. It's a state of oneness with pure consciousness.

In Advaita Vedanta, the world we perceive, with its multiplicity and distinctions, is a result of Māya (often translated as illusion or cosmic delusion). Māya causes the infinite and non-dual Brahman to appear as the diverse world. By realizing the निर्विकल्पं (Nirvikalpam) nature of Brahman, one transcends the veil of Māya and sees the undifferentiated reality. Such a Jnani (one who has realized the Self or Brahman) perceives the world without the constraints of conceptual distinctions. For the Jnani, everything is an expression of the non-dual Brahman. They see the underlying unity in all apparent dualities.

निर्विकल्पं (Nirvikalpam) is not just an intellectual understanding but a direct experience. The knowledge that arises from reading or hearing is termed परोक्ष ज्ञान (Parokṣa Jñāna – indirect knowledge). In contrast, the knowledge born out of direct experience is अपरोक्ष ज्ञान (Aparokṣa Jñāna – direct knowledge). Experiencing निर्विकल्पं (Nirvikalpam) is an instance of Aparokṣa Jñāna. It represents the essence of Brahman and points towards the state where all distinctions collapse, allowing the true, infinite nature of reality to shine forth. This concept challenges our everyday perceptions and encourages seekers to look beyond apparent dualities to perceive the underlying, unified nature of existence.

मायाकल्पितदेशकालकलनावैचित्र्यचित्रीकृतम्

māyākalpitadeśakālakalanāvaicitryacitrīkṛtam

The vastness and diversity of the universe is intricately crafted (citrīkṛtam) by the play of māyā, the cosmic illusion. This illusion introduces varied constructs of space (deśa) and time (kāla), creating a vast tableau of diverse experiences and phenomena (vaicitrya).

The phrase माया-कल्पित-देशकालकलना-वैचित्र्य-चित्रीकृतम् (māyā-kalpita-deśakālakalanā-vaicitrya-citrīkṛtam) conveys the idea that the variety and diversity of existence, as differentiated by space, time, and their multifaceted divisions, are all manifested or projected by Māyā.

Brahman, the ultimate reality, is timeless, spaceless, and non-dual. Yet, when viewed through the lens of Māyā, this singular reality appears as the diverse universe governed by space, time, and endless variations. The vast expanse of space, the linear progression of time, and the myriad entities and events they contain are all seen as projections or manifestations arising from Māyā.

For instance, imagine watching a film on a screen. The screen itself is unchanging, but the movie projected onto it presents diverse scenes, characters, and events. Similarly, Brahman is the immutable "screen," while the universe, with its spatial-temporal dimensions and countless diversities, is the "movie" projected by Māyā.

This concept challenges our regular perceptions, asserting that the reality we perceive — with its spatial dimensions, temporal progression, and variegated entities — is a construct of Māyā. The true nature of existence, according to Advaita Vedanta, is beyond these constructs and is singular, non-dual, and unchanging.

मायावीव विजृम्भयत्यपि महायोगीव यः स्वेच्छया
māyāvīva vijṛmbhayatyapi mahāyogīva yaḥ svechchhayā

The supreme consciousness, often equated to the ultimate Guru or God, is depicted here as a grand illusionist (māyāvī) and a great yogi (mahāyogī). Much like a magician unfolds a grand spectacle, or a yogi exercises his will, this supreme power manifests the universe (vijṛmbhayati) according to its own divine will (svechchhayā). This phrase encapsulates a profound idea about the nature of the universe and its creation.

The overarching idea here is that the universe's manifestation is not random or chaotic but is a deliberate and willed process, much like the intentional acts of a magician or a yogi. This willed process, however, is not to be attributed to a human-like deity but to the ineffable, infinite consciousness, Brahman, that underlies everything. The phrase accentuates the illusory nature of the universe and the immense underlying power or consciousness that brings it into apparent existence.

तस्मै श्रीगुरुमूर्तये नम इदं श्रीदक्षिणामूर्तये

tasmai śrīgurumūrtaye nama idaṁ śrīdakṣiṇāmūrtaye

The verse culminates with a salutation and offering of respect to the Guru, represented as Dakṣiṇāmūrti. This divine form is a personification of supreme knowledge and wisdom. Here, the reverence is directed towards this embodiment of eternal truth which guides seekers towards understanding the mysteries of the universe and the play of māyā.

In essence, the verse emphasizes the intricate and wondrous play of māyā that crafts the universe. The Guru, embodied as Dakṣiṇāmūrti, provides the wisdom and insight to comprehend this grand illusion and recognize the underlying unchanging truth.

यस्यैव स्फुरणं सदात्मकमसत्कल्पार्थकं भासते

साक्षात्तत्त्वमसीति वेदवचसा यो बोधयत्याश्रितान् ।

यत्साक्षात्करणाद्भवेन्न पुनरावृत्तिर्भवाम्भोनिधौ

तस्मै श्रीगुरुमूर्तये नम इदं श्रीदक्षिणामूर्तये ॥ ३ ॥

yasyaiva sphuraṇaṁ sadātmakam asat kalpārthakaṁ bhāsate

sākṣāttattvamasi iti vedavacasā yo bodhayaty āśritān I

yatsākṣātkaraṇādbhavenna punarāvṛttirbhavāmbhonidhau

tasmai śrīgurumūrtaye nama idaṁ śrīdakṣiṇāmūrtaye II 3 II

Word-by-word breakdown

यस्य एव स्फुरणं सत्-आत्मकम् असत्-कल्पार्थकं भासते
साक्षात् तत् त्वम् असि इति वेद-वचसा यः बोधयति आश्रितान् ।
यत्-साक्षात्करणात् भवेत् न पुनः आवृत्तिः भव-अम्भोनिधौ
तस्मै श्री-गुरु-मूर्तये नमः इदं श्री-दक्षिणा-मूर्तये ॥ ३ ॥

Yasya eva sphuraṇaṁ sat-ātmakam asat-kalpārthakaṁ bhāsate

Sākṣāt tat tvam asi iti veda-vacasā yaḥ bodhayati āśritān

Yat-sākṣāt-karaṇāt bhavet na punaḥ āvṛttiḥ bhava-ambhonidhau

Tasmai śrī-guru-mūrtaye namaḥ idaṁ śrī-dakṣiṇā-mūrtaye

II 3 II

Meaning

यस्यैव (yasyaiva): whose indeed; स्फुरणं (sphuraṇam): shining, manifestation; सत्-आत्मकम् (sat-ātmakam): having the nature of eternal essence; असत् (asat): unreal; कल्पार्थकं (kalpārthakam): imagination, having the meaning; भासते (bhāsate): shines; साक्षात् (sākṣāt): directly; तत् त्वम् असि इति (tat- tvam-asi-iti): "thou art that" thus; वेदवचसा (vedavachasā): with the voice of the Vedas; यः (yaḥ) = who; भोदयति (bhodayati): teaches, awakens; आश्रितान् (āśritān): the devoted, followers; यत् साक्षात्करणात् (yat sākṣātkaraṇāt): by whose realization; भवेत् (bhavet): may be; न (na): not; पुनरावृत्तिः (punarāvṛttiḥ): no return; भवाम्भोनिधौ (bhavāmbhonidhau): in the ocean of existence; तस्मै (tasmai): to that; श्रीगुरुमूर्तये (śrīgurumūrtaye): to the holy form of the Guru; नम (nama): salutation; इदं (idam): this; दक्षिणामूर्तये (śrīdakṣiṇāmūrtaye): to Shri Dakṣiṇāmūrti

> *Whose very manifestation illuminates the eternal self, making the unreal appear as if real,*
>
> *Who instructs his devotees with the Vedic statement 'You are that very Truth (Tattvamasi)'*
>
> *By whose direct realization there is no return to the ocean of worldly existence*
>
> *To that glorious Guru-form, I bow; to that revered Dakṣiṇāmūrti .*

Commentary

The verse praises the unchanging essence present in Sri Dakṣiṇāmūrti . He directly communicates the deep wisdom of "Thou art That," as voiced by the Vedas. When one realizes this, they are freed from the repetitive cycle of life and can distinguish reality from mere illusion. The verse wraps up with an acknowledgment of Shri Dakṣiṇāmūrti as the embodiment of the enlightened Guru.

भोदयति (bhodayati) is a verb that typically means "to make aware", "to inform", "to enlighten", or "to awaken someone to a certain knowledge or realization". The root भुद् (bhud) relates to "understanding" or "becoming aware." So, bhodayati can refer to the act of imparting understanding or realization.

This verse is a profound exposition of the nature of reality, the role of the Guru, and the essence of the Vedantic teachings. It speaks to the core principles of non-dualism, the ever-present consciousness, and the transcendental nature of the Guru. Let's delve deeper into its layers of meaning.

यस्यैव स्फुरणं सदात्मकमसत्कल्पार्थकं भासते

yasyaiva sphuraṇaṁ sadātmakamasatkalpārthakaṁ bhāsate

The phrase elucidates the radiant (sphuraṇaṁ) essence of the eternal truth (sadātmakam) which shines forth and renders the unreal (asat) or illusory perceptions (kalpārthakaṁ) manifest. This suggests the illuminating nature of the Absolute Truth that makes the ephemeral and transitory world apparent.

Here, sadātmakam refers to the true essence, the ultimate reality, or Brahman. सत् (Sat) has multiple meanings, including 'existence,' 'reality,' 'truth,' and 'that which is. आत्मकम् (Ātmakam) can be understood as 'nature' or 'essence.' When combined, सदात्मकम् (Sadātmakam) translates to "having the nature of existence" or "having the essence of reality/truth."

In the context of Advaita Vedanta, the term takes on a deeper, more profound meaning. "सत्" (Sat) represents the unchanging, eternal truth, which is in stark contrast to the transient and illusory world. It's one of the three primary characteristics of Brahman, the ultimate reality, as described in the Upanishads – Sat (existence), Chit (consciousness), and Ananda (bliss). So, when one speaks of something as सदात्मकम् (Sadātmakam), it means that the thing in question embodies the nature of this eternal, unchanging truth or existence. It is not transient, temporary, or illusory, but rather, it has the nature of the ultimate, undying reality.

असत् कल्पार्थकं भासते (asat-kalpārthakaṁ bhāsate) alludes to the apparent reality of the world (which is non-existent in its essence) seeming real due to Māyā.

Everything we perceive in this world is a manifestation or projection of Brahman, the ultimate reality. The ever-changing world of phenomena (names, forms, objects) is called "Māyā" and is considered unreal in the sense that it is transient and constantly changing. It is this Māyā that makes the non-existent (the illusory world of forms) seem real.

साक्षात्तत्त्वमसीति वेदवचसा यो बोधयत्याश्रितान्
sākṣāttattvamasīti vedavacasā yo bodhayatyāśritān

This segment refers to the sacred Vedic proclamation तत्त्वमसि (tat tvam asi) meaning "Thou art That". It is a declaration of one's true nature as the Universal Self. The Guru, through the words of the Vedas, enlightens (bodhayati) the disciples (āśritān) by imparting this profound knowledge.

तत्त्वमसि (Tattvamasi) is a phrase that stands as one of the foundational tenets of Advaita Vedanta. This phrase is one of the four Mahāvākyas, or "Great Sayings," of the

Upanishads. It means तत् (**Tat**): That; त्वम् (**Tvam**): You; असि (**Asi**): Are. When combined, "तत्त्वमसि" directly translates to "Thou art That" or more colloquially, "You are That."

The phrase तत्त्वमसि appears in the Chāndogya Upanishad, where the teacher Uddalaka Aruni instructs his son, Shvetaketu, using this statement as a recurrent theme to impart the knowledge of the ultimate reality.

The term points to the essence of individual existence and its relationship with the universe:

- तत् (**Tat**) - **That**: Refers to Brahman, the supreme, unchanging reality amidst and beyond the world. Brahman is the fundamental basis of all existence but transcends worldly understanding and definitions.

- त्वम् (**Tvam**) - **You**: Represents the individual self or Ātman. It refers to our inner self, our essence, the soul, or the spirit within each individual.

- असि (**Asi**) - **Are**: The verb that bridges the individual self and the universal reality, implying identity or oneness between them.

Tattvamasi suggests that the individual self (Ātman) is not different from the cosmic reality (Brahman). They are one and the same. This statement challenges the perception of duality, asserting that the seeming multiplicity and diversity of the world is an illusion, and in essence, everything is one singular reality.

Advaita Vedanta proposes that ignorance (Avidya) veils this truth from the average individual. But, when one realizes the essence conveyed by Tattvamasi, they break free from this illusion and understand their true nature. For the seeker of truth, understanding and internalizing this statement can be transformative. It implies that by realizing our true nature (Ātman), we recognize our identity with the broader, infinite reality (Brahman). Such realization leads to liberation (Mokśa), freeing one from the cycle of birth and death (Samsāra) and the suffering inherent in it.

Tattvamasi encapsulates the essence of Advaita Vedanta's teachings, emphasizing the non-dual nature of existence and urging us to recognize our deeper self, which is eternal and unified with the universal consciousness.

This part of the verse (in Dakṣiṇāmūrti Stotram) also underscores the importance of a guru or spiritual teacher. It suggests that it's the guru, grounded in the knowledge of the Vedas, who illuminates this profound truth to the seekers. By doing so, the guru helps dispel the ignorance that keeps individuals from recognizing their true nature. Through this enlightenment, seekers come to realize their oneness with the absolute reality, Brahman.

यत्साक्षात्करणाद्भवेन्न पुनरावृत्तिर्भवाम्भोनिधौ

yatsākṣātkaraṇādbhavenna punarāvṛttirbhavāmbhonidhau

This can be translated as: "By the direct realization of which, there is no repeated occurrence or rebirth in the ocean of worldly existence."

Through the direct realization (sākṣātkaraṇāt) of this supreme truth, as guided by the Guru, one does not get ensnared again (na punarāvṛttir) in the ocean of cyclical existence (bhavāmbhonidhau) or the cycle of birth and death.

The term भवाम्भोनिधौ (bhavāmbhonidhau) is a compound word (samāsa). भव (bhava) refers to the worldly existence or samsāra , often representing the cycle of birth and death, or the transient nature of life. आम्भोनिधौ (āmbhonidhau) can be further split into आम्भः (āmbhaḥ) = water and निधौ (nidhau) = in the reservoir or ocean. Bhavāmbhonidhau refers to "in the ocean of worldly existence" or "in the ocean of samsāra."

The term संसार (saṃsāra) means the cycle of birth, death, and rebirth, governed by karma. It symbolizes the worldly existence and the cyclical nature of life and death, characterized by suffering and impermanence. The ultimate goal if human life, according to Vedanta, is to transcend or break free from संसार (saṃsāra) and attain mokśa, signifying liberation or enlightenment.

The metaphor of the "ocean of worldly existence" (भव-आम्भो-निधौ, bhava-ambho-nidhau) is a powerful symbol used across various texts and hymns. This vast, tumultuous ocean represents Samsāra, the cycle of birth, death, and rebirth that souls are trapped within due to ignorance (Avidya) and their accumulated karma. Just as one may struggle to cross a vast, stormy ocean, souls entangled in Samsāra face numerous challenges, pains, and distractions that keep them from realizing their true nature.

However, the phrase suggests that by directly realizing or experiencing one's true nature (often identified as Brahman or the Universal Self), one can break free from this cycle. This realization is not just intellectual understanding but a profound, transformative experience that transcends thought. Once this experience or realization occurs, the individual no longer accrues karma that would lead to rebirth, and they achieve Mokśa or liberation from Samsāra.

In essence, the statement emphasizes the significance of self-realization. It suggests that true freedom from the pains and cycles of worldly existence comes not from external rituals, wealth, or worldly achievements, but from the profound inner realization of one's unity with the universal consciousness.

तस्मै श्रीगुरुमूर्तये नम इदं श्रीदक्षिणामूर्तये

tasmai śrīgurumūrtaye nama idaṁ śrīdakṣiṇāmūrtaye

The verse culminates with a veneration to the Guru, represented as Dakṣiṇāmūrti. This divine form of the Guru is a symbol of the ultimate consciousness and knowledge. Through these lines, deep respect and gratitude are offered to the Guru who reveals the path to self-realization.

The verse highlights the pivotal role of the Guru in illuminating the path to self-realization. Through the teachings of the Guru, the disciple understands the transitory nature of the world and recognizes their true self, thus freeing themselves from the endless cycle of birth and death. The salutation to Dakṣiṇāmūrti underscores the divinity and significance of the Guru in this spiritual journey.

नानाच्छिद्रघटोदरस्थितमहादीपप्रभाभास्वरं
ज्ञानं यस्य तु चक्षुरादिकरणद्वारा बहिः स्पन्दते ।
जानामीति तमेव भान्तमनुभात्येतत्समस्तं जगत्
तस्मै श्रीगुरुमूर्तये नम इदं श्रीदक्षिणामूर्तये ॥४॥

nānāchchhidraghaṭodarasthitamahādīpprabhā
bhāsvaraṁ
jñānaṁ yasya tu cakṣurādikaraṇadvāra bahiḥ spandate I
jānāmīti tameva bhāntamanubhātyetatsamastaṁ jagat
tasmai śrīgurumūrtaye nama idaṁ śrīdakṣiṇāmūrtaye II
4 II

Word-by-word breakdown

नाना च्छिद्र घट उदर स्थित महा दीप प्रभा भास्वरं
ज्ञानं यस्य तु चक्षुरादि करण द्वारा बहिः स्पन्दते ।
जानामीति तमेव भान्तम् अनुभात्य् एतत् समस्तं जगत्
तस्मै श्री गुरुमूर्तये नम इदं श्रीदक्षिणामूर्तये ॥४॥

nānā cchidra ghaṭa udara sthita mahā dīpa prabhā bhāsvaraṁ

jñānaṁ yasya tu cakṣurādi karaṇa dvārā bahiḥ spandate

jānāmīti tameva bhāntam anubhāty etat samastaṁ jagat

tasmai śrī gurumūrtaye nama idaṁ śrīdakṣiṇāmūrtaye II 4 II

Meaning

नानाच्छिद्र (nānācchidra): various holes; घटोदर (ghaṭodara): pot's belly (or cavity of a pot); स्थित (sthita): situated; महादीप (mahādīpa): great lamp; प्रभा (prabhā): light; भास्वरं (bhāsvaraṁ): luminous; ज्ञानं (jñānaṁ): knowledge; यस्य (yasya): whose; तु (tu): but; चक्षुरादि (cakṣurādi): eye etc. (sensory organs); करण (karaṇa): instrument; द्वारा (dvārā): through, by means of; बहिः (bahiḥ): outside; स्पन्दते (spandate): vibrates, functions; जानामीति (jānāmīti): "I know" thus; तमेव (tameva): that alone; भान्तं (bhāntaṁ): shining; अनुभाति (anubhāti): reflects; एतत् (etat): all this; समस्तं (samastaṁ): entire; जगत् (jagat): universe; तस्मै (tasmai): to that; श्रीगुरुमूर्तये (śrīgurumūrtaye): to the sacred form of the Guru; नम (nama): salutation; इदं (idaṁ): this; श्रीदक्षिणामूर्तये (śrīdakṣiṇāmūrtaye): to Shri Dakṣiṇāmūrti

Like the radiant light of a lamp situated within various perforated pots

The knowledge that, through organs like eyes, becomes manifest outside

That alone shines forth as 'I know', illuminating the entire universe

To that Shri Guru form, I offer my salutations, to that Shri Dakṣiṇāmūrti

Commentary

The meaning of this verse can be summarized as a comparison of the knowledge of the self to a lamp inside a pot with various holes (senses). This lamp allows the functioning of the senses, and the entire universe is illuminated by this knowledge. The verse concludes with a salutation to the divine form of Guru, Sri Dakṣiṇāmūrti.

The verse beautifully describes the inner light of consciousness that shines through all of us and illuminates the entire world. Just like a lamp placed inside a pot with holes can illuminate the surroundings, the inner consciousness shines. Everything we perceive, the knowledge of "I know", is due to this inner light. The verse then offers salutations to this embodiment of knowledge, represented by Sri Dakṣiṇāmūrti.

नानाच्छिद्रघटोदरस्थितमहादीपप्रभाभास्वरं

nānācchidraghaṭodarasthitamahādīpprabhābhāsvaram

This can be translated as: "The great lamp situated inside the pot, shining forth through the various holes." This phrase describes a metaphor. The imagery is of a large lamp (mahādīpa) placed inside a pot (ghaṭa) that has multiple holes (nānā-cchidra). The light from the lamp shines through these holes, just like consciousness illuminates our experiences through various senses.

In this metaphor, the "pot" represents the individual body-mind complex. Just as a pot might have various holes, the human system has multiple avenues through which it perceives and interacts with the world – these can be thought of as the senses and faculties. The "great lamp" inside the pot symbolizes the inner consciousness or the Self (Ātman).

The shining of the lamp's light through the pot's holes represents the manifestation of the one consciousness through individual bodies and minds. While the light (consciousness) is singular and undivided, when it shines through the various holes (individual senses and faculties), it appears as many.

The analogy beautifully encapsulates the non-dualistic teaching of Advaita Vedanta: while there appear to be many individual souls (Jīvātman) functioning in the world, they all derive their consciousness from the same source, the one Universal Self (Brahman or Paramātman).

In essence, this imagery serves to communicate the idea that while beings might appear distinct and separate due to their individual physical and mental compositions, at the core, they all share the same essence, the same luminous consciousness. It's a call to look beyond apparent differences and recognize the shared light within all.

ज्ञानं यस्य तु चक्षुरादिकरणद्वारा बहिः स्पन्दते
jñānaṁ yasya tu cakṣurādikaraṇadvārā bahiḥ spandate

The knowledge or awareness (jñānam) of that Supreme Reality operates through various instruments, like the eyes (cakṣu) and other sensory organs (ādikaraṇa). This consciousness manifests and interacts with the external world (bahiḥ) through these sensory gateways.

This statement touches on a central theme in many Indian philosophical systems: the nature of consciousness or awareness and its interaction with the external world. The "consciousness" or "knowledge" mentioned here can be understood as the internal, subjective experience of awareness. The sensory organs, starting with the eyes but also including the ears, nose, tongue, and skin, are the means through which this internal consciousness interacts with and perceives the external world.

When the phrase says the consciousness "functions externally," it's highlighting the outward-directed nature of our usual conscious experience. Typically, our awareness is directed outwards – we're conscious of sights, sounds, tastes, etc., of the world around us. This outward movement or functioning of consciousness is facilitated by the sensory organs.

In essence, the statement captures a fundamental human experience: our awareness, facilitated by our sensory organs, is typically directed at the external world. This recognition is often the first step in many spiritual paths that subsequently guide seekers to explore the source and nature of this consciousness.

जानामीति तमेव भान्तमनुभात्येतत्समस्तं जगत्

jānāmīti tameva bhāntamanubhātyetatsamastaṁ jagat

This phrase translates to, "That alone which manifests as 'I know' illumines the entire world."

The entire universe (samastaṁ jagat) is illuminated by that same consciousness, and it is by this consciousness that one gets the sense of "I know" (jānāmīti). This self-awareness and knowledge of the external world are both manifestations of that underlying, all-pervading consciousness.

The statement starts with the acknowledgment of the awareness "I know." This simple, foundational aspect of consciousness – the knowingness, the awareness – is given primacy. It's the light by which everything else is known.

The phrase then asserts that this consciousness or the feeling of "I know" is what illumines or makes known the entire world (samastaṁ jagat, समस्तं जगत्). This is to say, our entire experience of the world is mediated through our consciousness. The world is known to us only because it's illuminated by our awareness.

Such observations underscore the indivisible nature of consciousness. The world isn't separate from consciousness but arises within and is known by it. The distinction between the knower, the process of knowing, and the known is blurred, leading to the assertion of a non-dual reality where consciousness is the fundamental substrate.

In essence, this statement underscores the foundational role of consciousness in our experience of the world. The world is known because it shines in the light of our awareness. This reflection on the relationship between consciousness and the world can lead to deeper philosophical inquiries into the nature of reality, the self, and the universe.

तस्मै श्रीगुरुमूर्तये नम इदं श्रीदक्षिणामूर्तये

tasmai śrīgurumūrtaye nama idaṁ śrīdakṣiṇāmūrtaye

The verse culminates with a salutation to the Guru, embodied as Dakṣiṇāmūrti. This form of the Divine Guru is symbolic of that ultimate consciousness and knowledge. Through these lines, one offers their respects and gratitude to this representation of wisdom and understanding.

The verse uses vivid imagery to describe how the singular, unchanging consciousness permeates our varied experiences, both internal and external. It underscores the omnipresence of this consciousness, and how our understanding and experiences are but reflections of this primal knowledge. The salutation to Dakṣiṇāmūrti underscores the role of the Guru in helping seekers realize this profound truth.Top of Form

देहं प्राणमपीन्द्रियाण्यपि चलां बुद्धिं च शून्यं विदुः
स्त्रीबालान्धजडोपमास्त्वहमिति भ्रान्ता भृशं वादिनः ।
मायाशक्तिविलासकल्पितमहाव्यामोहसंहारिणे
तस्मै श्रीगुरुमूर्तये नम इदं श्रीदक्षिणामूर्तये ॥५॥

deham prāṇamapīndriyāṇyapi ca calām buddhim ca
śūnyam viduḥ

strībālāndhajaḍopamāstvahamiti bhrāntā bhṛśam vādinaḥ I

māyāśaktivilāsakalpitamahāvyāmohasamhāriṇe

tasmai śrīgurumūrtaye nama idam śrīdakṣiṇāmūrtaye II 5 II

Word-by-word breakdown

देहं प्राणम् अपि इन्द्रियाणि अपि चलाम् बुद्धिम् च शून्यं विदुः
स्त्री-बाल-अन्ध-जड-उपमाः तु अहम् इति भ्रान्ताः भृशं वादिनः ।
माया-शक्ति-विलास-कल्पित महा-व्यामोह-संहारिणे
तस्मै श्री-गुरु-मूर्तये नमः इदं श्री-दक्षिणामूर्तये ॥५॥

deham prāṇam api indriyāṇi api calām buddhim ca
śūnyam viduḥ

strī-bāla-andha-jaḍa-upamāḥ tu aham iti bhrāntāḥ bhṛśam
vādinaḥ

māyā-śakti-vilāsa-kalpita mahā-vyāmoha-samhāriṇe

tasmai śrī-guru-mūrtaye namaḥ idam śrī-dakṣiṇāmūrtaye II 5 II

Meaning

देहं (deham): body; प्राणम (prāṇam): life, vital breath; अपि (api): also; इन्द्रियाणि (indrīyāṇi): senses; अपि (api): also; चलां (calām): moving; बुद्धिं (buddhim): intellect; च (ca): and; शून्यं (śūnyam): void; विदुः (viduḥ): know; स्त्री (strī): woman; बाल (bāla): child; अन्ध (andha): blind; जडोपमाः (jaḍopamāḥ): comparable to the inert; तु (tu) indeed; अहम्-इति (aham iti): "I am that," thus; भ्रान्ताः (bhrāntāḥ): deluded; भृशं (bhṛśam): very much; वादिनः (vādinaḥ): argumentative; माया-शक्ति-विलास (māyā-śakti-vilāsa): the play of the power of illusion; कल्पित (kalpita): imagined; महा-व्यामोह (mahā-vyāmoha): great delusion; संहारिणे (saṃhāriṇe): the destroyer; तस्मै (tasmai): to that; श्रीगुरुमूर्तये (śrīgurumūrtaye): to the sacred form of the Guru; नम (nama): salutation; इदं (idam): this; श्रीदक्षिणामूर्तये (śrīdakṣiṇāmūrtaye): to Shri Dakṣiṇāmūrti

People recognize the body, breath, senses, moving mind, and even intellect as themselves;

They argue vehemently that 'I' is nothing but likened to women, children, and the blind.

To Him, who destroys this great delusion caused by the playful power of Māya,

To that form of the divine Guru, I offer my salutations – to Sri Dakṣiṇāmūrti.

Commentary

The essence of this verse speaks to those who are deluded, equating themselves with their body, breath, senses, intellect, and void. This delusion makes them comparable to women, children, and the blind, who are symbolized as unaware or innocent of true wisdom. The verse praises Shri Dakṣiṇāmūrti, the divine form of the Guru, as the destroyer of this great delusion, which is born from the play of the power of illusion.

This verse deals with multiple themes: the nature of self-identification, the nature of worldly illusion (māyā), and the significance of the Guru in spiritual understanding. Each line can be examined for its deeper philosophical insights:

देहं प्राणमपीन्द्रियाण्यपि चलां बुद्धिं च शून्यं विदुः

dehaṁ prāṇamapīndriyāṇyapi calāṁ buddhiṁ ca śūnyaṁ
viduḥ

The verse starts by listing the elements many mistakenly identify with: the body (deham), life force or prāṇa, senses (indriyāṇi), the fickle mind (calāṁ buddhim), and even the void or nothingness (śūnya). These are the conventional identifications most individuals adhere to in their understanding of 'self.'

These terms देहं (dehaṃ): body; प्राणम (prāṇam): life, vital breath; इन्द्रियाणि (indriyāṇi): senses; बुद्धिं (buddhiṃ): intellect; and शून्यं (śūnyaṃ): void, need some explanation to understand their nature of Ātman.

The term देहं (deham) refers to the physical body, which is the material form that houses the individual's consciousness. In this philosophical framework, the concept of देहं (deham) serves to emphasize the impermanence of the physical body and encourages individuals to recognize their true nature beyond the material realm. The teachings of Vedanta aim to lead individuals towards self-realization, where they can transcend identification with the physical body and realize their essential nature as part of the greater reality.

In the context of Indian philosophy, प्राण (prana) refers to the vital life force or energy that permeates and sustains all living beings. It is the animating force that is responsible for all life processes and activities. Prana is often described as the universal life energy that flows through everything in the cosmos, connecting all living entities.

There are five main types of prāṇa, collectively known as the "Pancha Prāṇa" or "Five Vital Airs." These prāṇa regulate various physiological and psychological functions within the human body. Each prana has its own specific role and location in the human body:

1. प्राण (prāṇa): This is the upward-moving life force associated with the breath of inhalation. It governs the functions related to the upper body, including respiration, circulation, and sensory perceptions. Prana is also connected to vitality, energy, and enthusiasm.

2. अपान (apāna): Apana is the downward-moving prana associated with the breath of exhalation. It

controls elimination, excretion, and reproduction. Apana is responsible for the functions of the lower abdomen and pelvic region.

3. व्यान (vyāna): Vyana prana circulates throughout the entire body and is responsible for the coordination of various bodily functions. It facilitates the movement of energy, helps maintain balance, and ensures the harmonious interaction of the other prāṇa.

4. उदान (udāna): Udana prana is associated with the upward movement of energy, particularly in the throat region. It is responsible for actions such as speech, expression, growth, and spiritual aspirations. Udana is also connected to the process of dying and departing from the body.

5. समान (samāna): Samana prana operates in the region around the navel and is responsible for digestion, assimilation, and the equitable distribution of energy and nourishment throughout the body. It ensures that the body's systems work together harmoniously.

The understanding and harmonious balance of these prāṇa are considered crucial for maintaining physical health, mental clarity, and spiritual growth in various Indian spiritual and philosophical traditions, including Yoga, and Ayurveda.

In the present context, realizing that prana is distinct from Ātman is crucial. While prana is the energy that sustains life processes, such as breathing, circulation, and bodily functions, it is considered a part of the physical and energetic aspects of the individual. Ātman, on the other hand, is the concept of the individual self or soul. It is the eternal, unchanging essence that is beyond the physical body and mind. Ātman is considered the true self that transcends the temporary nature of the physical world.

While both prana and Ātman are both non-material concepts, they refer to different aspects of the human experience. Prana pertains to the life force and energy that animate the body, while Ātman relates to the deeper, eternal essence of the individual self. In Vedanta, realizing the true nature of Ātman and its connection to the ultimate reality (Brahman) is a central goal.

The term इन्द्रियाणि (Indriyāṇi) refers to the sense organs in the human body and represents the faculties through which we perceive and interact with the external world. And the terms ज्ञानेन्द्रियाणि (jñānendriyāṇi) and कर्मेन्द्रियाणि (karmendriyāṇi) refer to two different categories of sense organs that play specific roles in our perception.

1.   ज्ञानेन्द्रियाणि (Jnana Indriyāṇi) - These are the sense organs of knowledge or perception. There are five Jnana Indriyas, corresponding to the five senses:

   •   श्रोत्रम् (śrotram) - The ear, responsible for receiving auditory stimuli and hearing.

- चक्षु (Cakṣu) - The eye, responsible for perceiving visual information and seeing.
- घ्राण (Ghrāṇa) - The nose, responsible for detecting smells and olfactory sensations.
- जिह्वा (Jihvā) - The tongue, responsible for experiencing tastes and gustatory sensations.
- त्वक् (Tvak) - The skin, responsible for feeling touch and tactile sensations.

These sense organs allow us to gather information from the external world, which is processed by the mind to create our sensory experiences.

2. कर्मेन्द्रियाणि (karmendriyāṇi) - These are the organs of action. There are also five karmendriyās:

- वाक् (vāk) - The organ of speech, responsible for communication and expression.
- पाणि (pāṇi) - The hands, responsible for activities like grasping, holding, and manipulating objects.
- पाद (pāda) - The feet, responsible for walking and movement.
- पायु (pāyu) - The excretory organ, responsible for eliminating waste from the body.
- उपस्थ (upastha) - The reproductive organ, responsible for procreation.

These organs allow us to interact with the world physically through actions and movements.

In essence, Jnana Indriyas help us perceive the world, while Karma Indriyas facilitate our interaction with the world through actions. In ayurveda, balancing and directing the senses can contribute to overall well-being and inner growth. In spiritual practices, understanding the roles of these sense organs is important for developing self-awareness, self-control, and mindfulness. While the senses can lead to distractions, they are not inherently negative. When they are harnessed and balanced, they can be tools for experiencing the world while keeping a connection to the deeper self (Ātman).

In the context of Vedanta, the relationship between Indriyas and Ātman involves recognizing the role of the senses in human experience while simultaneously understanding that the true self is beyond the sensory world. The spiritual journey often involves transcending the influence of the senses and realizing the unchanging essence of the Ātman. Top of Form

बुद्धि (Buddhi) is a concept that plays a significant role in understanding the human mind and its relationship to the higher self, आत्मन् (Ātman). Buddhi is part of Antahkāraṇa, that is involved in cognition.

Antahkāraṇas refer to the inner faculties of the mind, consisting of four components: **Manas** (mind), **Buddhi** (intellect), **Chitta** (memory or subconscious), and **Ahamkara** (ego). Each component has its own function, and together they form the inner psychological framework that shapes human experience.

Buddhi is often translated as "intellect" or "discerning faculty." It represents the aspect of the mind that processes information, evaluates, discriminates, judges, and makes decisions. Buddhi is responsible for logical reasoning, analysis, and determining right from wrong. It's the part of the mind that helps you understand concepts, analyze situations, and make informed choices.

In relation to **Ātman**, the individual self or soul, the interaction can be understood as follows:

Buddhi and Ātman Distinction: Buddhi is a part of the inner psychological apparatus, whereas Ātman is considered the eternal, unchanging essence of the individual. Buddhi operates within the realm of thoughts and experiences, while Ātman transcends these fluctuations.

Identifying with the Mind: The challenge for individuals is that they often identify themselves primarily with their thoughts, emotions, and intellect (Buddhi). This identification can lead to a sense of separateness, suffering, and ego-driven behaviors.

Realizing the Ātman: The spiritual journey involves recognizing the distinction between the changing nature of the mind and the unchanging nature of the Ātman. Through practices like meditation, self-inquiry, and detachment from the fluctuations of the mind, one can start to experience the deeper essence of the self.

Harmonious Relationship: While Buddhi can lead to confusion and attachment when not properly understood, it also has the potential to be a tool for self-realization. When Buddhi is directed towards self-inquiry and seeking the truth, it can aid in transcending the limitations of the mind and realizing the oneness with the higher self (Ātman).

In summary, **Buddhi** is a key component of the mind that performs cognitive functions, and its relationship with the **Ātman** involves recognizing the distinction between the changing nature of the mind and the unchanging essence of the self. The journey of self-realization involves going beyond the fluctuations of the Buddhi and connecting with the deeper truth of the Ātman.

शून्यं (śūnyaṃ) is a term associated with Buddhist philosophy, and it translates to "emptiness" or "voidness" in English. But the translation of शून्यं (śūnyaṃ) as "emptiness" or "voidness" is not accurate. While these translations are commonly used to convey the general idea, the concept of शून्यं (śūnyaṃ) in Buddhist philosophy is more nuanced than simply denoting an empty or void state.

शून्यं (śūnyaṃ) in Buddhist philosophy, particularly in the Mahayana tradition, refers to the "emptiness of inherent existence." It signifies the absence of intrinsic, independent, and unchanging nature in all phenomena, including the ego-self. This concept challenges the idea of selfhood and permanence in the conventional sense.

The term "emptiness" doesn't imply a complete void or nothingness, but rather points to the interdependent and interconnected nature of all things. It suggests that phenomena lack self-existence and can only be understood in relation to other phenomena. It is a profound concept that goes beyond a simple absence or void.

Translations can sometimes struggle to capture the full depth and subtleties of philosophical ideas, especially when they come from languages with different cultural and philosophical contexts. It's always recommended to explore the original term and its nuances in its native context to fully understand its intended meaning

In Buddhist philosophy, the realization of emptiness is a path to liberation from suffering. It suggests that by recognizing the emptiness of all things, individuals can overcome attachment, desire, and the cycle of suffering (samsāra). शून्यं (śūnyaṃ) emphasizes the impermanent and interconnected nature of reality, questioning the substantial existence of entities as they are conventionally perceived.

While शून्यं (śūnyaṃ) and आत्मन् (Ātman) are two different concepts, and they can be seen as contradicting each other within certain philosophical contexts. The apparent contradiction between these concepts is a point of discussion and debate, particularly between different philosophical schools in Indian thought.

The contradiction arises primarily between Buddhist philosophy, which emphasizes the idea of "emptiness" (śūnyatā) and denies the inherent existence of self, and certain schools of Indian philosophy like Vedanta, which emphasize the existence of an eternal self (Ātman) as the core essence of an individual.

In Buddhist philosophy, particularly in the Mahayana tradition, the concept of śūnyaṃ (emptiness) is central. It challenges the idea of a permanent, unchanging self and asserts that all phenomena lack inherent existence. This includes the denial of a permanent individual self (Ātman). The realization of emptiness is considered essential for liberation from suffering.

In contrast, Vedanta and related philosophies emphasize the existence of आत्मन् (Ātman) as an eternal, unchanging essence that transcends the material world. The realization of one's true self (Ātman) is seen as a path to self-realization and unity with the ultimate reality (Brahman).

Various scholars and philosophers have attempted to reconcile or bridge the gap between these seemingly contradictory views. Some suggest that the concepts might be pointing to different aspects of reality or might be different paths to the same truth. Others propose that they are addressing different levels of understanding or are suited for different individuals with varying spiritual inclinations.

Ultimately, the apparent contradiction between शून्यं (śūnyaṃ) and आत्मन् (Ātman) reflects the diversity and richness of Indian philosophical thought. Different schools offer distinct perspectives on the nature of reality and the path to liberation. While they may seem contradictory, exploring these concepts can lead to a deeper understanding of the complexities of existence and the nature of the true self.

This line of the verse points to a profound truth about the nature of the self and the world. It suggests that those who gain true wisdom understand that the body, breath, senses, and even the restless mind are impermanent and ever-changing. This realization leads to a deeper understanding of the transient nature of the physical world and the illusory nature of sensory experiences. This part of the verse invites seekers to look beyond the transient and illusory aspects of existence and discover the deeper truth that leads to self-realization and spiritual awakening.

स्त्रीबालान्धजडोपमास्त्वहमिति भ्रान्ता भृशं वादिनः

strībālāndhajaḍopamāstvahamiti bhrāntā bhṛśaṃ vādinaḥ

Many argue vehemently (bhṛśaṃ vādinaḥ) that the self is like (upamā) a woman, child, blind, or inert (strī-bāla-andha-jaḍa). This showcases the varied misconceptions and misunderstandings about the nature of self, comparing it with ephemeral or limited entities, and reflects the depth of their delusion (bhrāntā). This verse emphasizes the delusions of those who identify themselves with their physical bodies, gender, age, and intellect, while remaining oblivious to the deeper truth of their own existence.

Here's a simple explanation of the verse:

- स्त्रीबालान्धजडोपमाः (Stri-Bala-Andha-Jada-Upamah) - This phrase points to the comparison of individuals to women (stri), children (bala), and the blind (andha), indicating those who are deeply engrossed in the material world, lack discernment, and are unaware of their true nature. It symbolizes people who prioritize the transient aspects of life.

- त्वहमिति भ्रान्ताः (tvahamiti bhrāntāḥ) - तु indeed; अहम्-इति (aham iti): "I am that," thus; भ्रान्ताः (Bhraantah) refers to being deluded or mistaken. This part of the verse implies that these individuals are under the illusion that they are the physical body, mind, intellect, and ego. They wrongly identify themselves solely with their external appearances, roles, and worldly attributes.

- भृशं वादिनः (Bhrisham Vaadinah) - भृशं (Bhrisham) means "excessively," and वादिनः (Vaadinah) refers to those who engage in argumentation or intellectual debates. This part of the verse characterizes those who are learned and well-versed in various discussions but remain entrapped in the cycle of arguments without grasping the essence of self-realization.

This part of the verse reflects on the prevalent condition of humanity, where individuals are engrossed in their worldly roles and identities. They are consumed by their external appearances, roles, and intellectual pursuits, unaware of their true nature. This points to the idea that true wisdom comes not from external knowledge alone but from recognizing the unchanging essence that transcends the transient aspects of life.

Adi Shankaracharya uses these concepts to highlight the need for self-discovery. He encourages individuals to go beyond mere intellectual debates and to realize the deeper truth of their existence. It's a call to recognize one's identity beyond the limitations of the body, age, gender, and intellect, and to realize the unchanging, eternal essence within.

मायाशक्तिविलासकल्पितमहाव्यामोहसंहारिणे

māyāśaktivilāsakalpitamahāvyāmohasaṁhāriṇe

The illusionary power of māyā creates this great confusion (mahāvyāmoha) regarding the true nature of self. However, there exists a force or energy that can dispel (saṁhāriṇe) this grand illusion. This energy helps in transcending these misconceptions and misidentifications.

Here is a break down the phrase to understand its significance in more detail:

- माया (Māya) शक्तिविलास (Shakti-Vilasa): Māya is a fundamental concept in Indian philosophy, representing the cosmic illusion that veils the true nature of reality. It creates a sense of separation between the individual and the ultimate truth. Shakti-Vilasa refers to the play or manifestation of divine power. शक्ति (Shakti) signifies the creative power of the universe, and विलास (Vilasa) indicates the expression or display of this power.

- कल्पित (Kalpita): This word means "imagined" or "conceived." It refers to the way in which Māya projects the world as we perceive it, creating an illusory reality.

- महाव्यामोहसंहारिणे (Mahavyamoha-Samharine): महा (Maha) means great, व्यामोह (Vyamoha) signifies delusion, and संहारिणे (Samharine) means destroyer. This part of the phrase emphasizes the role of Lord Dakṣiṇāmūrti as the destroyer of the great delusion caused by Māya.

In Advaita Vedanta, Māya is often understood in terms of two primary aspects: आवरणशक्ति (Āvarana Shakti) and विक्षेपशक्ति (Vikśepa Shakti). These Sanskrit terms represent the functions of Māya in concealing the ultimate reality and projecting the world of appearances. Let's explore these concepts in detail:

- आवरणशक्ति (Āvarana Shakti):
    - आवरण (Āvarana) translates to "covering" or "veiling."
    - शक्ति (Shakti) means "power" or "energy."
    - Āvarana Shakti is the power of Māya that veils or covers the true nature of Brahman, the ultimate reality. It acts as a curtain that obscures the non-dual nature of existence and presents a distorted perception of reality.
    - It is this aspect of Māya that prevents individuals from recognizing their true divine nature and keeps them entangled in the illusion of duality and multiplicity.
    - Āvarana Shakti is like a mist that obscures the clear view of the absolute reality, making it difficult to perceive the unity that underlies all apparent diversity.
- विक्षेपशक्ति (Vikśepa Shakti):
    - विक्षेप (Vikśepa) translates to "projection" or "displacement."
    - शक्ति (Shakti) again refers to "power" or "energy."
    - Vikśepa Shakti is the power of Māya that projects the diverse world of names and forms. It is the force through which the formless Brahman appears as the multitude of objects and beings in the manifested universe.

- This aspect of Māya creates the illusion of individuality, objects, relationships, and the entirety of the manifest world.

- Vikśepa Shakti is like a magician's trick, creating an illusion of separateness and diversity where, in reality, there is only the underlying unity of Brahman.

Together, Āvarana Shakti and Vikśepa Shakti represent the dual functioning of Māya in creating the illusory world. Āvarana Shakti veils the ultimate reality, while Vikśepa Shakti projects the world of appearances. The combination of these two aspects keeps individuals bound to the cycle of samsāra (worldly existence) by perpetuating the belief in a separate self and an external world.

The spiritual path in Advaita Vedanta involves transcending these dual aspects of Māya through self-inquiry, meditation, and realization of one's true nature as non-dual Brahman. By understanding and directly experiencing the illusory nature of Māya, seekers can break free from its grip and attain self-realization and liberation (mokśa).

This phrase शक्तिविलासकल्पितमहाव्यामोहसंहारि णे (śakti-vilāsa-kalpita mahā-vyāmoha-samhāriṇe) expresses the idea that Māya's play creates a vast web of illusory experiences that trap individuals in ignorance. It acknowledges the potency of Māya's power to create extensive delusion, making individuals perceive the world as separate from the ultimate reality. In summary, this phrase encapsulates the essence of the Dakṣiṇāmūrti Stotram, which emphasizes the importance of seeking spiritual knowledge to overcome the illusions of the material world.

तस्मै श्रीगुरुमूर्तये नम इदं श्रीदक्षिणामूर्तये

tasmai śrīgurumūrtaye nama idaṁ śrīdakṣiṇāmūrtaye

The verse concludes with a salutation to the Guru, embodied in the form of Dakṣiṇāmūrti, the universal teacher. This Guru, or the Supreme Teacher, is the one who can dispel the misconceptions created by māyā and guide individuals towards the realization of their true nature.

The verse beautifully portrays the myriad ways in which individuals misidentify their true nature, attributing it to the body, mind, void, and other temporal entities. It emphasizes the role of the Guru, represented by Dakṣiṇāmūrti, in guiding the individual out of these delusions and towards self-realization.

राहुग्रस्तदिवाकरेन्दुसदृशो मायासमाच्छादनात्

सन्मात्रः करणोपसंहरणतो योऽभूत्सुषुप्तः पुमान् ।

प्रागस्वाप्समिति प्रबोधसमये यः प्रत्यभिज्ञायते

तस्मै श्रीगुरुमूर्तये नम इदं श्रीदक्षिणामूर्तये ॥ ६॥

Rāhugrastadivākarendusadṛśo māyāsamācchādanāt
Sanmātraḥ karaṇopasaṃharaṇato yo'bhūtsuṣuptaḥ
pumān |
Prāgasvāpsamiti prabodhasamaye yaḥ pratyabhijñāyate
Tasmai śrīgurumūrtaye nama idaṃ śrīdakṣiṇāmūrtaye II
6 II

Word-by-word breakdown

राहुग्रस्त-दिवाकर-इन्दु-सदृश: माया-समाच्छादनात्
सन्मात्रः करण-उप-संहरणत: यः अभूत-सुषुप्तः-पुमान् ।
प्राक्-अस्वाप्सम्- इति प्रबोध-समये यः प्रति-अभिज्ञायते
तस्मै श्री-गुरु-मूर्तये नमः इदं श्री-दक्षिणा-मूर्तये ॥ ६॥

rāhugrasta-divākara-indu-sadṛśaḥ māyā-samācchādanāt

sanmātraḥ karaṇa-upa-saṃharaṇataḥ yaḥ abhūta-
suṣuptaḥ-pumān

prāk-asvāpsam iti prabodha-samaye yaḥ prati-abhijñāyate

tasmai śrī-guru-mūrtaye namaḥ idaṃ śrī-dakṣiṇā-mūrtaye

II 6 II

Meaning

राहुग्रस्त (rāhugrasta): seized by Rahu (a reference to an eclipse); दिवाकर (divākara): sun; इन्दु (indu): moon; सदृश: (sadṛśaḥ): similar to; माया-समा-छादनात् (māyā-samā-chādanāt): by the covering of illusion; सन्मात्रः (sanmātraḥ): merely existence; करणोपसंहरणत: (karaṇopa saṃharaṇataḥ): from the withdrawal of the senses; यः अभूत् (yaḥ abhūt): who became; सुषुप्तः (suṣuptaḥ): in deep sleep; पुमान्

(pumān): person; प्राक्-अस्वाप्सम्- इति (prāk-asvāpsam-iti): Before I was asleep; प्रबोधसमये (prabodhasamaye): at the time of awakening; यः (yaḥ): who; प्रत्यभिज्ञायते (pratyabhijñāyate): is recognized; तस्मै (tasmai): to Him; श्रीगुरुमूर्तये (śrīgurumūrtaye): to the sacred form of the Guru; नम (nama): salutation; इदं (idaṃ): this; श्रीदक्षिणामूर्तये (śrīdakṣiṇāmūrtaye): to Shri Dakṣiṇāmūrti

> *Just as the Sun and Moon are obscured by the eclipse caused by Rahu,*
>
> *In the same way, the pure consciousness is obscured by the illusion of Māyā.*
>
> *This being in deep sleep, where only the pure existence remains without senses,*
>
> *And is the same that is recognized as 'I' upon awakening.*
>
> *To that form of the auspicious Guru, to Sri Dakṣiṇāmūrti, I offer my salutations*

Commentary

This verse describes how a person in deep sleep is obscured by the veil of illusion, just as the sun and moon are obscured by Rahu during an eclipse. Upon awakening, the true self is recognized as merely existing, akin to the realization that the sun and moon were there all along, just hidden. The verse ends with a salutation to Shri Dakṣiṇāmūrti, the embodiment of the Supreme Guru, who is the one that grants this realization.

राहुग्रस्तदिवाकरेन्दुसदृश: मायासमाच्छादनात्
rāhugrasta-divākara-endu-sadṛśaḥ māyā-samācchādanāt

The translation of this statement would be: "Like the sun and moon eclipsed by Rahu, (the Self) is obscured by Māyā." The verse begins with a vivid imagery. The sun and the moon, despite being luminous celestial entities, are occasionally eclipsed by Rahu, a shadow entity. The luminosity is never truly gone, but merely obscured. This analogy points to our true nature or the self (Ātman) which, though inherently pure and luminous, seems to get eclipsed or obscured by ignorance (avidyā).

In this context, Rahu is a shadowy celestial entity in Vedic astrology, responsible for causing eclipses. When Rahu seizes the sun or the moon, we experience solar or lunar eclipses, respectively. During this period, the true luminosity of these celestial bodies is obscured from our view. Similarly, the verse indicates that the true nature of our Self (or Ātman) is obscured by Māyā.

As mentioned earlier, Māyā, in Advaita Vedanta, is the cosmic force of illusion that makes the absolute reality (Brahman) appear as the diverse world (Jagat) to our senses. It veils the true nature of the Self and projects multiplicity. Just as the eclipse temporarily veils the luminosity of the sun or moon, Māyā veils our true self, which is pure consciousness.

In summary, the verse captures the essence of Advaita Vedanta by drawing a parallel between the temporary obscurance of celestial luminaries by an eclipse and the obscuring of our true self by the illusionary power of Māyā. It emphasizes the need for spiritual knowledge to lift this veil and realize one's true nature.

सन्मात्रः करण-उप-संहरणतः यः अभूत-सुषुप्तः-पुमान्

sanmātraḥ karaṇa-upa-saṁharaṇataḥ yaḥ abhūta-
suṣuptaḥ-pumān

This verse addresses the state of deep sleep, one of the three primary states of human experience according to Advaita Vedanta – the other two being the waking (jāgrat) and dream (svapna) states.

In the deep sleep state (suṣupti), there is a complete withdrawal of the sensory and motor organs, and the individual is devoid of any dualistic experiences or perceptions. There are no dreams, no sense of 'I', no external world – just pure existence or being. This state is often taken as an analogy in Advaita Vedanta to describe the nature of the ultimate reality, Brahman, which is pure consciousness devoid of attributes.

The phrase सन्मात्रः करण-उप-संहरणतः (sanmātraḥ karaṇa-upa-saṁharaṇataḥ) suggests that in deep sleep, due to the withdrawal of the sensory and motor organs, what remains is just the 'mere existence' or the 'pure being'. It indicates the dormant state where the play of māyā (duality, differentiation) temporarily ceases. Yet, the self continues to exist.

अभूत-सुषुप्तः-पुमान् (abhūta-suṣuptaḥ-pumān) indicates the person in the deep sleep state where he did not become anything, implying that he did not take on any roles, identities, or experiences. He was just pure existence without any attributes.

This verse draws attention to the deep sleep state to elucidate the nature of the Self (Ātman) and its identity with Brahman. Just as in deep sleep, where only pure existence prevails without any dualistic experiences, the ultimate nature of the Self is pure consciousness, without attributes or dualities. The deep sleep state serves as an experiential pointer towards understanding the non-dual nature of reality.

This is a continuation from the previous line, emphasizing the existence of the individual during deep sleep. Although there's no active cognition of the external world or inner mental world during this state, one still exists in pure form.

प्रागस्वाप्समिति प्रबोधसमये यः प्रत्यभिज्ञायते

prāgasvāpsam-iti prabodha-samaye yaḥ pratyabhijñāyate

Upon waking from deep sleep, there's an innate understanding or recognition that "I slept well" or "I was unaware of anything." This shows a continuity of consciousness. Even though one was not actively aware during sleep, the consciousness remains unchanged and recognizes the state of rest upon waking.

This statement has profound philosophical implications related to the nature of consciousness and the continuous sense of self. Despite the various states of consciousness that a person undergoes (like waking, dreaming, and deep sleep), there exists a continuous, unchanging sense of self or consciousness that remains consistent throughout these states.

For instance, when we wake up from sleep, we often recall or recognize our experiences from the previous day or the dreams we might have had. There's an inherent knowledge or recognition of the continuity of our self, even though the states (wakefulness, dream, deep sleep) are different. This recognition hints at the unchanging, underlying nature of the self or consciousness, which is a pivotal idea in Advaita Vedanta.

The concept stresses the existence of an underlying, unchanging consciousness that remains as a constant witness throughout the various states and experiences of life. This Self is said to be identical with the universal consciousness, Brahman, and realizing this identity is the ultimate goal of Advaita Vedanta.

तस्मै श्रीगुरुमूर्तये नम इदं श्रीदक्षिणामूर्तये

tasmai śrī-guru-mūrtaye nama idaṁ śrī-dakṣiṇā-mūrtaye

The verse concludes with a salutation to the Guru, epitomized as Dakṣiṇāmūrti, a form of Lord Shiva that represents the supreme teacher. The Guru, through the teachings of Advaita Vedanta, illuminates the disciple's mind, dispelling the darkness of ignorance. Just as one recognizes their state of deep sleep upon waking, through the guidance of the Guru, one recognizes their true self — Ātman which is Brahman.

The verse, in essence, guides us through a journey of self-realization, from understanding the obscuring nature of māyā, experiencing our true self in deep sleep, and recognizing this upon awakening, and ultimately seeking refuge in the wisdom of the Guru, who is the embodiment of the supreme knowledge and truth.

बाल्यादिष्वपि जाग्रदादिषु तथा सर्वास्ववस्थास्वपि
व्यावृत्तास्वनुवर्तमानमहमित्यन्तः स्फुरन्तं सदा ।
स्वात्मानं प्रकटीकरोति भजतां यो मुद्रयाभद्रया
तस्मै श्रीगुरुमूर्तये नम इदं श्रीदक्षिणामूर्तये ॥७॥

Bālyādiṣvapi jāgradādiṣu tathā sarvāsvavasthāsvapi

Vyāvṛttāsvanuvartamānamahamityantaḥ sphurantaṁ sadā

Svātmānaṁ prakaṭīkaroti bhajatāṁ yo mudrayābhadrayā

Tasmai śrīgurumūrtaye nama idaṁ śrīdakṣiṇāmūrtaye ॥7॥

Word-by-word breakdown

बाल्यादिषु अपि जाग्रदादिषु तथा सर्वासु अवस्थासु अपि
व्यावृत्तासु अनुवर्तमानम् अहम् इति अन्तः स्फुरन्तं सदा ।
स्वात्मानं प्रकटीकरोति भजतां यः मुद्रया भद्रया
तस्मै श्री -गुरु-मूर्तये नमः इदं श्री-दक्षिणामूर्तये ॥७॥

bālyādiṣu api jāgradādiṣu tathā sarvāsu avasthāsu api
vyāvṛttāsu anuvartamānam aham iti antaḥ sphurantaṁ sadā
svātmānaṁ prakaṭīkaroti bhajatāṁ yaḥ mudrayā bhadrayā
tasmai śrī-guru-mūrtaye namaḥ idaṁ śrī-dakṣiṇāmūrtaye II 7 II

Meaning

बाल्यादिषु-अपि (bālyādiṣu api): (Amongst) in childhood and other stages, also; जाग्रदादिषु (jāgradādiṣu): In wakefulness, etc.; तथा (tathā): Similarly; सर्वासु-अवस्थासु-अपि (sarvāsu avasthāsu api): In all states; व्यावृत्तासु-अनुवर्तमानम् (vyāvṛttāsu-anuvartamānam): Following after what has passed; अहं-इति-अन्तः (aham-iti-antaḥ): The idea of 'I' within; स्फुरन्तं (sphurantam): Shining; सदा (sadā): Always; स्वात्मानं (svātmānam): One's own Self; प्रकटीकरोति (prakaṭīkaroti): Makes manifest; भजतां (bhajatām): To the devoted; यः (yaḥ): Who; मुद्रयाभद्रया (mudrayābhadrayā): With the bhadra (auspicious) mudra (seal or gesture); तस्मै (tasmai): To that; श्रीगुरुमूर्तये (śrīgurumūrtaye): To the sacred form of the Guru; नम (nama): Salutation; इदं (idam): This; श्रीदक्षिणामूर्तये (śrīdakṣiṇāmūrtaye): To Shri Dakṣiṇāmūrti

In all the stages, from childhood and so on, in all the states of wakefulness and so forth,

And in all conditions, the internal notion of 'I' always shines forth.

To the devotees, He makes this very Self apparent through the auspicious gesture (mudra).

To that Śrī Guru in the form of Dakṣiṇāmūrti, I offer my salutations.

Commentary

This verse acknowledges that the idea of 'I' shines within all states of life, from childhood to wakefulness, following what has passed but always present. This realization of one's own Self is made manifest to those who are devoted by Shri Dakṣiṇāmūrti, who is depicted with the auspicious mudra. The verse concludes with a salutation to Shri Dakṣiṇāmūrti, the embodiment of the Supreme Guru.

बाल्यादिष्वपि जाग्रदादिषु तथा सर्वास्ववस्थास्वपि
bālyādiṣvapi jāgradādiṣu tathā sarvāsvavasthāsvapi

The phrase can be interpreted as: "In all stages, starting from childhood and in all states of consciousness, beginning with the waking state." This means that irrespective of the various life stages (like childhood, youth, and old age) and states of consciousness (waking, dreaming, and deep sleep), there is an unchanging, underlying principle or consciousness that remains as a constant witness. This is a central tenet of Advaita Vedanta.

It emphasizes that while external conditions and internal states might change, there is an eternal, unchanging essence or Ātman that persists unchanged. This Ātman is beyond the realms of time, space, and causation, and realizing its true nature, which is identical with the universal Brahman.

व्यावृत्तास्वनुवर्तमानमहमित्यन्तः स्फुरन्तं सदा

vyāvṛttāsvanuvartamānamahamityantaḥ sphurantaṁ sadā

The phrase can be interpreted as: "The 'I' or Self, which is distinct from the external, continuously manifests and shines eternally within."

Despite the constant change and evolution in external circumstances and inner experiences, there remains a constant and uninterrupted inner awareness or consciousness — the innate sense of "I am". This eternal presence persistently shines forth, irrespective of external or internal variations.

This highlights several foundational principles of self-realization:

1. **Distinction of the Self from the External**: The Self (or Ātman) is distinct from the body, mind, and external world. It's not entangled in the transient events of the external realm. The "external" here

refers to all that is anātmā (non-self) – the body, mind, sensory perceptions, and worldly objects.

2. **Constant Manifestation**: The Self continuously shines or reveals itself. Unlike objects that appear and disappear, the true nature of the Self is ever-present.

3. **Inner Illumination**: The Self is self-luminous. Just as the Sun doesn't require another light to be seen, the Self illuminates itself and doesn't depend on external factors for its recognition.

4. **Eternal Presence**: The nature of the Self is eternal. It's not bound by time and remains unchanged across past, present, and future.

The overarching message here is the constant and self-evident nature of the Ātman or Self. While the external world is characterized by change, flux, and transience, the Ātman remains unchanged, ever-present, and self-luminous. Realizing this Ātman as one's true identity and understanding its distinction from the external world is a central aim of self-realization.

स्वात्मानं प्रकटीकरोति भजतां यो मुद्रयाभद्रया

svātmānaṁ prakaṭīkaroti bhajatāṁ yo mudrayābhadrayā

The phrase can be translated as: "That (divine entity or principle) which, with an auspicious gesture (mudra), reveals or manifests the true Self to those who worship (or adore) it."

The Guru, through symbolic gestures (mudras) and teachings, reveals this ever-present Self to the devoted seekers. The Guru, with benevolent grace, makes evident the eternal Self that remains unchanged across life's varying states.

The phrase points to the process of self-realization. The true nature of an individual, the Ātman, is often obscured by ignorance and worldly distractions. The spiritual journey involves recognizing and realizing this true Self. The act of revealing the self is often not a mere individual effort. Divine grace, symbolized by the benevolent mudra, plays a significant role. The auspicious gesture or mudra here can signify a particular blessing or an act of grace that aids in the realization.

Those who worship or adore the divine principle with sincerity and devotion (भजतां, bhajatām) are the recipients of this revelation. This underscores the significance of Bhakti or devotion as a path to self-realization.

The phrase captures the essence of a seeker's journey, emphasizing the union of individual effort (devotion) and divine grace in realizing one's true nature.

तस्मै श्रीगुरुमूर्तये नम इदं श्रीदक्षिणामूर्तये

tasmai śrī-guru-mūrtaye nama idaṁ śrī-dakṣiṇā-mūrtaye

The verse culminates in an expression of deep reverence and gratitude to the Guru, embodied as the form of Dakṣiṇāmūrti, the quintessential teacher aspect of Lord Shiva. By illuminating the disciple's understanding, the Guru reveals the true nature of the Self, which remains steadfast amidst the ever-changing states of existence.

In essence, this verse eloquently captures the unwavering presence of the Self amidst life's vicissitudes and the pivotal role of the Guru in revealing this perennial truth to sincere seekers.

विश्वं पश्यति कार्यकारणतया स्वस्वामिसम्बन्धतः
शिष्याचार्यतया तथैव पितृपुत्राद्यात्मना भेदतः ।
स्वप्ने जाग्रति वा य एष पुरुषो मायापरिभ्रामितः
तस्मै श्रीगुरुमूर्तये नम इदं श्रीदक्षिणामूर्तये ॥८॥

Viśvaṁ paśyati kāryakāraṇatayā svasvāmisambandhataḥ

śiṣyācāryatayā tathaiva pitṛputrādyātmanā bhedataḥ |

Svapne jāgrati vā ya eṣa puruṣo māyāparibhrāmitaḥ

Tasmai śrīgurumūrtaye nama idaṁ śrīdakṣiṇāmūrtaye ||8||

Word-by-word breakdown

विश्वं पश्यति कार्यकारणतया स्व-स्वामि-सम्बन्धतः
शिष्य-आचार्यतया तथैव पितृ-पुत्राद्यात्मना भेदतः ।
स्वप्ने जाग्रति वा यः एषः पुरुषः माया-परिभ्रामितः
तस्मै श्री-गुरु-मूर्तये नमः इदं श्री-दक्षिणामूर्तये ॥८॥

viśvaṁ paśyati kārya-kāraṇa-tayā sva-svāmi-
sambandhataḥ

śiṣya-ācārya-tayā tathaiva pitṛ-putrādy-ātmanā bhedataḥ

svapne jāgrati vā yaḥ eṣaḥ puruṣaḥ māyā-paribhrāmitaḥ

tasmai śrī-guru-mūrtaye namaḥ idaṁ śrī-dakṣiṇāmūrtaye

|| 8 ||

Meaning

विश्वं (viśvaṃ): The universe; पश्यति (paśyati): Sees; कार्य-कारण-तया (kārya-kāraṇa-tayā): As the effect and cause; स्व-स्वामि-सम्बन्धतः (sva-svāmi-sambandhataḥ): In the relationship of servant and master; शिष्याचार्यतया (śiṣyācāryatayā): In the relationship of student and teacher; तथैव (tathaiva): Likewise; पितृ-पुत्रादि-आत्मना (pitṛu-putrādi-ātmanā): In the relationship of father and son, etc.; भेदतः (bhedataḥ): In differentiation; स्वप्ने (svapne): In dream; जाग्रति (jāgrati): In wakefulness; वा (vā): Or; एष (eṣa): This; पुरुषो (puruṣo): Person; मायापरिभ्रामितः (māyāparibhrāmitaḥ): Deluded by illusion; तस्मै (tasmai): To that; श्रीगुरुमूर्तये (śrīgurumūrtaye): To the sacred form of the Guru; नम (nama): Salutation; इदं (idaṃ): This; श्रीदक्षिणामूर्तये (śrīdakṣiṇāmūrtaye): To Shri Dakṣiṇāmūrti

He sees the universe in terms of cause and effect,

In terms of the relationship between master and servant,

In terms of the relationship between teacher and disciple,

*And in terms of other relationships, like that between
father and son.*

*In dreams and in waking, this individual is deluded by
illusion (māyā).*

*To that divine teacher in the form of Dakṣiṇāmūrti, I offer
my salutations.*

Commentary

This verse elucidates the way people perceive the universe
as a play of cause and effect, seeing relationships such as
servant and master, student and teacher, father and son,
and so on. These perceptions create differentiation and
occur both in the dream state and wakefulness. All of these
perceptions are expressions of delusion caused by Māya,
the cosmic illusion. The verse concludes with a salutation
to Shri Dakṣiṇāmūrti, who embodies the Supreme Guru
and transcends these illusions.

विश्वं पश्यति कार्यकारणतया स्वस्वामिसम्बन्धतः

viśvaṁ paśyati kāryakāraṇatayā svasvāmi-sambandhataḥ

The world or the cosmos is perceived in terms of cause
and effect. We consistently attempt to explain the universe
in terms of reasons and outcomes. This dichotomous
view has a beginning in duality and separateness, not
recognizing the underlying unity of existence.

शिष्याचार्यतया तथैव पितृपुत्राद्यात्मना भेदतः

śiṣyācāryatayā tathaiva pitṛputrādyātmanā bhedataḥ

Relationships are seen in various forms like master-servant, teacher-student, father-son, etc., each emphasizing the differences and separations. These relational dynamics often tether one to the realm of duality and miss the fundamental oneness that pervades all relationships.

स्वप्ने जाग्रति वा य एष पुरुषो मायापरिभ्रामितः

svapne jāgrati vā ya eṣa puruṣo māyā-paribhrāmitaḥ

Whether in a dream or in the waking state, the individual soul (puruṣa) is deluded and led astray by māyā, the cosmic illusion. Māyā creates a sense of separateness and veils the true nature of reality, causing the soul to perceive diversity and differences.

तस्मै श्रीगुरुमूर्तये नम इदं श्रीदक्षिणामूर्तये

tasmai śrī-guru-mūrtaye nama idaṁ śrī-dakṣiṇā-mūrtaye

This segment of the verse offers salutations to the Guru embodied as Dakṣiṇāmūrti, a manifestation of Lord Shiva representing supreme knowledge. The Guru, akin to Dakṣiṇāmūrti, illuminates the path, dispelling the veils of māyā and guiding the seeker towards the realization of the underlying unity in all perceived diversities.

In summary, this verse discusses the different perspectives through which an individual perceives the world and its relationships. At the outset, the world is viewed through the lens of cause and effect. This is expanded upon by further looking at various relational dynamics, including those between the self and its master, the student and teacher, and familial ties like that between a father and son.

These relationships and perceptions manifest across different states of consciousness — specifically, the waking and dream states. However, the underlying theme is the concept of Māyā, the illusory force that deludes the soul and shapes these perceptions.

Despite the multifaceted nature of our experiences and the illusions that come with them, there exists a constant and unchanging truth. This truth is embodied in the form of the Guru, who is a manifestation of universal consciousness. The Guru acts as a beacon, guiding souls through the maze of Māyā towards enlightenment.

The verse culminates in a profound acknowledgment and veneration of Dakshinamurthy, the cosmic teacher who represents this ultimate wisdom and clarity amidst the chaos of worldly perceptions.

भूरम्भांस्यनलोऽनिलोऽम्बरमहर्नाथो हिमांशु पुमान्
इत्याभाति चराचरात्मकमिदं यस्यैव मूर्त्यष्टकम् ।
नान्यत् किञ्चन विद्यते विमृशतां यस्मात्परस्मादविभोः
तस्मै श्रीगुरुमूर्तये नम इदं श्रीदक्षिणामूर्तये ॥९॥

Bhūrambhāṁsyanalo'nilo'ambaramaharnātho himāṁshu pumān
ityābhāti carācarātmakamidaṁ yasyaiva mūrtyaṣṭakam
nānyat kiñcana vidyate vimṛśatāṁ yasmātparasmādvibhoḥ
tasmai śrīgurumūrtaye nama idaṁ śrīdakṣiṇāmūrtaye ||9||

Word-by-word breakdown

भूः अम्भांस्य अनलः अनिलः अम्बरम् अहः नाथः हिमांशुः पुमान्

इति आभाति चर-अचर-आत्मकम् इदं यस्य एव मूर्ति-अष्टकम् ।
न अन्यत् किञ्चन विद्यते विमृशतां यस्मात् परस्मात् विभोः
तस्मै श्री-गुरु-मूर्तये नमः इदं श्री-दक्षिणामूर्तये ॥९॥

bhūḥ ambhāṁsy analaḥ anilaḥ ambaram ahaḥ nāthaḥ himāṁśuḥ pumān

iti ābhāti cara-acara-ātmakam idaṁ yasya eva mūrti-aṣṭakam

na anyat kiñcana vidyate vimṛśatāṁ yasmāt parasmāt vibhoḥ

tasmai śrī-guru-mūrtaye namaḥ idaṁ śrī-dakṣiṇāmūrtaye II 9 II

Meaning

भूः (Bhūḥ) – Earth; अम्भांस्य (Ambhāṁsya) – of water; अनलः (Analaḥ) – Fire; अनिलः (Anilaḥ) - Wind or air; अम्बरम् (Ambaram) - Sky; अहः-नाथः (Ahaḥ-Nāthaḥ) - The Lord or protector of day (the Sun); हिमांशुः (Himāṁśuḥ) - The moon (literal translation: 'cool-rayed', often referring to the moon's soothing light); पुमान् (Pumān) – person or Jīva-atma; इति (Iti) - Thus, this; आभाति (Ābhāti) - Appears or shines forth; चर-अचर-आत्मकम् (Chara-Achara-Ātmakam) -

Consisting of the moving and unmoving entities; इदं (Idaṃ) – This; यस्य (Yasya) – Whose; एव (Eva) – Indeed; मूर्ति-अष्टकम् (Mūrti-Aṣṭakam) - The group of eight forms; न (Na) – Not; अन्यत् (Anyat) – Another; किञ्चन (Kiñcana) – Anything; विद्यते (Vidyate) – Exists; विमृशतां (Vimṛśatāṃ) - Of those who contemplate or examine; यस्मात् (Yasmāt) - From whom; परस्मात् (Parasmāt) - Beyond, transcendent; विभोः (Viboḥ) - The almighty or supreme; तस्मै (Tasmai) - To him; श्री-गुरु-मूर्तये (Śrī-Guru-Mūrtaye) - To the sacred form of the Guru; नमः (Namaḥ) - Salutations or homage; इदं (Idaṃ) – This; श्री-दक्षिणामूर्तये (Śrī-Dakṣiṇāmūrtaye) - To Lord Dakṣiṇāmūrti

The Earth, Water, Fire, Air, Space, the Sun, the Moon, and the living being (Jīva) – this eightfold form manifests as both the animate and inanimate in this universe, and all these emerge from Him alone.

Upon introspection, nothing else is found to exist apart from the Supreme Sri.

To that Supreme Guru, who is beyond all, to Him, the embodiment of Sri Dakshinamurty, I offer my salutations.

Commentary

This verse describes the cosmic form of Sri Dakṣiṇāmūrti, an aspect of Shiva as the universal teacher. It lists the essential elements of Earth, Water, Fire, Air, Sky, and the Great Being, which shine forth as the forms of the cosmos. The author proclaims that nothing else is known to the contemplative sages besides these aspects of the Divine, and the verse concludes with a salutation to Sri Dakṣiṇāmūrti, the embodiment of cosmic wisdom.

भूरम्भांस्यनलोऽनिलोऽम्बरमहर्नाथो हिमांशु पुमान्

bhūrambhāṁsyanalo'nilo'ambaramaharnātho himāṁshu pumān

The verse starts by enumerating eight forms or aspects: Earth (bhū), Water (ambha), Fire (anala), Air (anila), Ether (ambaram), Day (ahaḥ), the Moon (himāṁshu), and the Jīva-atma (pumān). These eight entities symbolize the tangible and intangible aspects of the world we interact with. In philosophical contexts, they represent how the ultimate reality or divine manifests in the perceivable universe.

इत्याभाति चराचरात्मकमिदं यस्यैव मूर्त्यष्टकम्

ityābhāti carācarātmakamidaṁ yasyaiva mūrtyaṣṭakam

The moving (chara) and non-moving (achara) entities of the world manifest from these eight forms. They are manifestations of the Divine, arising from His (Its) octet of forms. This speaks to the idea that everything, from the grand expanse of the universe to the minutest entity, emanates from and is a reflection of the Divine's multifaceted nature.

नान्यत् किञ्चन विद्यते विमृशतां यस्मात्परस्मादविभो:

nānyat kiñcana vidyate vimṛśatāṁ yasmāt-parasmād-vibhoḥ

Upon contemplation and introspection, one realizes that apart from this Supreme Being, there is truly nothing else that exists. The multitude of forms and entities are but reflections and manifestations of that One Supreme Reality. This line emphasizes the non-dual nature of reality, where all perceived differences merge into one ultimate truth.

तस्मै श्रीगुरुमूर्तये नम इदं श्रीदक्षिणामूर्तये
tasmai śrī-guru-mūrtaye nama idaṁ śrī-dakṣiṇā-mūrtaye

The verse concludes by offering salutations to the Guru, embodied as Dakṣiṇāmūrti. The Guru, as the representative of the ultimate reality, serves as the bridge connecting the individual soul to the Supreme Reality. Through the teachings and grace of the Guru, the seeker is guided towards understanding and realizing the non-dual nature of existence.

This verse beautifully presents the idea that all of existence, in its myriad forms, is a manifestation of one Supreme Reality. Through the guidance of the Guru and introspection, one can pierce through the veil of apparent multiplicity to recognize and realize the underlying unity.

सर्वात्मत्वमिति स्फुटीकृतमिदं यस्मादमुष्मिन् स्तवे
तेनास्य श्रवणात्तदर्थमननाद्ध्यानाच्च संकीर्तनात् ।
सर्वात्मत्वमहाविभूतिसहितं स्यादीश्वरत्वं स्वतः
सिद्ध्येत्तत्पुनरष्टधा परिणतं चैश्वर्यमव्याहतम् ॥१०॥

Sarvātmatvamiti sphuṭīkṛtamidaṁ yasmādamuṣmin stave

tenāsya śravaṇāttadarthamananāddhyānācca saṅkīrtanāt |

Sarvātmatvamahāvibhūtisahitaṁ syādīśvaratvaṁ svataḥ

siddhyettatpunaraṣṭadhā pariṇataṁ

caisvaryamavyāhatam ||10||

Word-by-word breakdown

सर्व-आत्मत्वम् इति स्फुटीकृतम् इदं यस्मात् अमुष्मिन् स्तवे
तेन अस्य श्रवणात् तत् अर्थ मननात् ध्यानात् च संकीर्तनात् ।
सर्व-आत्मत्व महा-विभूति सहितं स्यात् ईश्वरत्वं स्वतः
सिद्ध्येत् तत् पुनः अष्टधा परिणतं च ऐश्वर्यम् अव्याहतम् ॥१०॥

sarva-ātmatvam iti sphuṭīkṛtam idaṁ yasmāt amuṣmin stave

tena asya śravaṇāt tat-artha mananāt dhyānāt ca saṁkīrtanāt

sarva-ātmatva mahā-vibhūti sahitaṁ syāt īśvaratvaṁ svataḥ

siddhyet tat punaḥ aṣṭadhā pariṇatam ca aiśvaryam

avyāhatam II 10 II

Meaning

सर्व आत्मत्वम् इति (sarva ātmatvam iti): The state of being the Self of all; स्फुटीकृतम् इदं (sphuṭīkṛtam idam) - Clearly explained this; यस्मात् अमुष्मिन् (yasmāt amuṣmin) - Because of which in this; स्तवे (stave) - In the stotram; तेन अस्य (tena asya) - By its; श्रवणात् (śravaṇāt) – Hearing; तत् अर्थ मननात् (tat-artha-mananāt) - Reflection on its meaning; ध्यानात् च (dhyānāt cca) - And meditation; संकीर्तनात् (saṃkīrtanāt) - And recitation; सर्वात्मत्वम् महाविभूतिसहितं (sarvātmatvam mahāvibhūtisahitam) - Being the self of all with great glory; स्यात् (Syāt) – would be or is ईश्वरत्वं (Īśvaratvaṃ) – lordship or divinity; स्वतः (svataḥ) – Naturally; सिद्ध्येत् तत् पुनः अष्टधा (Siddhyet tat punaḥ aṣṭadhā) - That becomes perfected eightfold; परिणतं च ऐश्वर्यम् अव्याहतम् (Parinatam cha aiśvaryam avyāhatam) - Uninterrupted glory transformed

The universal Selfhood is clearly expounded in this stotram; by its listening, reflecting on its meaning, meditating, and singing praises,

The realization of being the Universal Self, endowed with supreme powers, naturally culminates in the natural state of divinity.

Once this realization is achieved, it transforms into eightfold unobstructed divine attributes.

Commentary

This verse explains that through the clear exposition of the state of being the Self of all, one can attain that realization by hearing, reflecting on its meaning, meditation, and recitation. By doing so, one naturally becomes endowed with a state of divinity and an uninterrupted eightfold glory.

सर्वात्मत्वमिति स्फुटीकृतमिदं यस्मादमुष्मिन् स्तवे

sarvātmatvamiti sphuṭīkṛtamidaṁ yasmādamuṣmin stave

The essence of the entire hymn or Stotram is to expound the concept of 'sarvātmatva', which means the 'Self in all' or the universal selfhood. It suggests that the supreme reality is immanent in all things, living and non-living.

तेनास्य श्रवणात्तदर्थमननाद्ध्यानाच्च संकीर्तनात्

tenāsya śravaṇāttadarthamananāddhyānācca saṅkīrtanāt

By listening (śravaṇa) to this Stotram, reflecting (manana) upon its meaning, meditating (dhyāna) upon it, and singing (saṅkīrtanāt) its praises, one is guided toward realizing its essence. These practices enhance the spiritual aspirant's understanding, making the profound truths accessible and experientially real.

सर्वात्मत्वमहाविभूतिसहितं स्यादीश्वरत्वं स्वतः

sarvātmatvamahāvibhūtisahitaṁ syādīśvaratvaṁ svataḥ

Upon this realization of the all-pervading Self, one simultaneously recognizes the magnificent manifestations (mahāvibhūti) of the Divine in all things. This, in turn, naturally leads to an inherent sense of 'īśvaratva' or divinity within oneself. One doesn't become God but realizes their true nature as not separate from the Divine.

सिद्ध्येत्तत्पुनरष्टधा परिणतं चैश्वर्यमव्याहतम्
siddhyettatpunaṣṭadhā pariṇataṁ caisvaryamavyāhatam

This realization further matures and manifests as eight-fold unparalleled, unobstructed divine glories or 'aisvaryas'. These refer to spiritual siddhis or perfections that arise from deep realization, but they stand uncontested and pure, devoid of ego or attachment. These are the natural outcomes of recognizing one's divinity and the divinity of all. Here, the author is referring to ashta siddhis or eight accomplishments. These siddhis are considered extraordinary abilities that a practitioner may develop as they progress along their spiritual journey. The eight siddhis are:

1. **Aṇimā (अणिमा)**: Anima is the ability to become infinitely small or atomic in size. Those who possess this siddhi can reduce their physical body to the tiniest particle, allowing them to pass through solid objects effortlessly.

2. **Mahimā (महिमा)**: Mahima is the opposite of Anima. It is the ability to expand one's physical body to a vast size. Practitioners with this siddhi can become as large as they desire, even larger than mountains or celestial bodies.

3. **Laghimā (लघिमा)**: Laghima is the power to become extremely light, almost weightless. This siddhi allows one to levitate or float in the air effortlessly.

4. **Garimā (गरिमा):** Garima is the opposite of Laghima. It is the power to become incredibly heavy and dense. Those with this siddhi can increase their weight significantly.

5. **Prāpti (प्राप्ति):** Prapti is the ability to acquire or attain anything one desires, regardless of distance or obstacles. Practitioners with this siddhi can instantly reach or possess objects, even if they are far away.

6. **Prākāmya (प्राकाम्य):** Prakamya is the power to fulfill any desire or wish. It allows practitioners to have their desires instantly realized without any hindrance.

7. **īśitva (ईशित्व):** Ishitva is the power of supreme control or rulership. Those with this siddhi can have absolute authority and mastery over various aspects of the world, including elements and beings.

8. **Vaśitva (वशित्व):** Vashitva is the power to control and manipulate other beings or entities. Practitioners with this siddhi can subdue or influence others' actions and thoughts according to their will.

It's important to note that in Vedantic tradition, the pursuit of siddhis is not the ultimate goal of spiritual practice. While these powers can be developed, they are often seen as distractions from the path of spiritual realization and may even lead to egoism if not approached with humility and wisdom. True spiritual growth is often believed to involve transcending attachment to these siddhis and realizing one's essential nature, which is beyond such powers.

In summary, the verse emphasizes the transformative power of understanding one's inherent connection with the all-pervading Divine. Through listening, reflection, meditation, and praise, this understanding blossoms, leading to profound realizations and divine manifestations in one's life. This realization bestows divine qualities upon the seeker, culminating in the acquisition of eight forms of divine attributes and unbroken sovereignty. It underscores the transformative power of spiritual knowledge and practice in realizing one's true divine nature.

IAST Transliteration Key

IAST stands for "International Alphabet of Sanskrit Transliteration." The purpose of IAST is to provide a standardized and consistent way to write Sanskrit and Indic scripts using Roman letters, making it easier for people who are not familiar with the native scripts to read and pronounce words accurately.

IAST assigns specific diacritical marks and conventions to indicate Sanskrit sounds that do not have direct equivalents in the Roman alphabet. This system helps preserve the phonetic accuracy and pronunciation of Sanskrit words when transliterated into Roman characters. It is commonly used in academic and scholarly contexts for writing Sanskrit texts, as well as for teaching and publishing materials related to Sanskrit and other Indic languages.

अ	a	as in sun	क	K	*cut/kite*	ट	ṭa	*touch*
आ	ā	*Bald*	ख	kha	Book-*house*, 'k' combined with aspiration 'h'	ठ	ṭha	an*th*ill
इ	i	B*i*t	ग	Ga	Gun	ड	ḍa	*Dull*
ई	ī	B*ea*t	घ	gha	Pi*g-h*ead, the sound 'g' in 'gun' with aspiration 'h'.	ढ	ḍha	Go*dh*ead, aspiration as above
उ	u	P*u*t	ङ	ṅa	Lu*ng*	ण	ṇa	u*n*der (retroflex)
ऊ	ū	T*oo*l	च	Ca	*Ch*unk	त	Ta	Pa*th*
ऋ	ṛ	*Rhy*thm	छ	cha	cat*ch*-hold	थ	tha	The sound 'th' in '*th*umb' combined with aspiration 'h'
ए	e	*Date*	ज	Ja	*J*ug	द	Da	*Then*
ऐ	ai	*Might*	झ	Jha	He*dg*eh*og*, 'j' with aspiration	ध	dha	The sound 'th' in '*th*us' plus aspiration
ओ	o	*Oat*	ञ	Ña	B*un*ch	न	Na	*Number*
औ	au	*Out*						

प	pa	*Pot*	य	Ya	Yet	ष	ṣa	*sh*un
फ	pha	*Sou*p*-hu*nt, aspiration as above	र	Ra	*Run*	स	Sa	Sun
ब	ba	*But*	ल	La	*Love*	ह	ha	*H*all
भ	bha	*Ab*hor, aspiration as above	व	Va	Voice	क्ष	kṣa, combines the 'k' in 'king' with the sound 'sh' in *Shaw*	Ri*k*shaw
म	ma	Much	श	Śa	Sat	ज्ञ	Jña